UNIT 10

INTERNAL AND EXTERNAL FINANCE

Financial Strategy

Prepared for the Course Team by Janette Rutterford,
Mary Bowerman, Graham Francis and Marcus Davison

OPEN UNIVERSITY COURSE TEAM

Core Group

Professor Janette Rutterford, *Production and Presentation Course Team Co-Chair and Author*
David Barnes, *Author*
Bernardo Bátiz-Lazo, *Presentation Course Team Co-Chair and Author*
Marcus Davison, *Author*
Graham Francis, *Author*
Jan Gadella, *Author*
Margaret Greenwood
Heinz Kassier
Tony Anthoni, *Course Manager*
Clare Minchington, *Author*
Pat Sucher, *Author*
Patricia Swannell, *Author*
Richard Wheatcroft, *Author*

External Assessor

Professor Paul Draper, *Walter Scott and Partners Professor of Finance, University of Edinburgh*

Production Team

Sylvan Bentley, *Picture Researcher*
John Bradley, *Design Group Co-ordinator*
Martin Brazier, *Graphic Designer*
Henry Dougherty, *Editor*
Jenny Edwards, *Product Quality Assistant*

Anne Faulkner, *Information Specialist*
John Garne, *Computing Consultant*
Roy Lawrance, *Graphic Artist*
David Libbert, *BBC Series Producer*
Richard Mole, *Director of Production OUBS*
Kathy Reay, *Course Team Assistant*
Linda K. Smith, *Project Controller*
Doreen Tucker, *Compositor*
Steve Wilkinson, *BBC Series Producer*

External Critical Readers

Stephen Abbott
George Buckberry
Linda Cinderey
Roland Davis
Angela Garrett
Jane Hughes
Rosemary F. Johnson
Robin Joy
David Kirk
Archie McArthur
Richard Mischak
Eugene Power
Manvinder Singh
Tony Whitford
Chris Worthington

EVA® is a registered trademark of Stern Stewart

The Open University,
Walton Hall, Milton Keynes MK7 6AA

First published 1999. Second edition 1999. Third edition 2000. Reprinted 2002

Edited, designed and typeset by The Open University

Printed in the United Kingdom by The Burlington Press, Foxton, Cambridge CB2 6SW.

ISBN 0 7492 97891

Further information on Open University Business School courses may be obtained from the Course Sales Development Centre, The Open University, PO Box 222, Milton Keynes MK7 6YY (Telephone: 01908 653449).

oubs.open.ac.uk

3.4

26991B/b821b5u10i3.4

CONTENTS

1	Introduction		5
2	Corporate governance		10
	2.1	Market-based systems	10
	2.2	Relationship-based systems	14
		Summary	17
3	Internal v. external reporting		18
	3.1	Management and financial accounting	18
	3.2	Trends in performance measurement	21
	3.3	Economic and accounting performance measures	25
		Summary	39
4	Audit and Accountability in the Public Sector		40
	4.1	Definitions of value-for-money auditing	42
	4.2	The future of value-for-money auditing	54
	4.3	Best value	55
		Summary	56
5	Performance measurement and investment		58
	5.1	Measurement of trustee performance	58
	5.2	Measurement of fund manager performance	63
		Summary	70
	Summary and conclusions		71
	Answers to exercises		73
	References		74
	Acknowledgements		77

1 INTRODUCTION

In this final unit of B821 we examine in detail how the principles and techniques of finance are used in practice as a means of *controlling* an organisation.

When we discussed the language of finance in Unit 1 we stressed the need for care in the use of terms whose technical meanings differ subtly from their everyday meanings. 'Control' is one such term. In a financial context it has not one but two distinct meanings. In the active sense it means to direct, in just the same sense as when you control a car you tell it where to go and how fast. Control in this sense is something you do *before* and *during* the events you are controlling. But in finance it also has a more passive sense, which may not be so apparent in its everyday usage, that of keeping tabs on what is going on or of checking up on events afterwards. These are things you do *during* and *after* the events you are controlling. So financial control is both about making things happen and about finding out what is happening or has already happened.

Different languages strike different balances between these two ingredients in the idea of control. The German 'Kontrolle', for instance, stresses the element of checking up after the event. There is a well-known saying in German management circles: 'Vertrauen ist gut; Kontrolle ist besser', or 'Trust is good, but control is better.' This does not mean that it is better to drive the car yourself than to employ a driver, but rather that it is better to have a structured reporting and audit mechanism than just to trust your subordinates blindly.

BOX 1.1 CHAIN OF COMMAND

Financial control can also be understood as a kind of chain. An analogy is the chain of command in the military context, whereby orders are passed from the highest level of strategic decision-making to the lowliest foot-soldier at the front, and situation reports are fed back in the opposite direction. We all know what happens if the chain is broken or if orders or reports become garbled in transmission.

In a famous (but probably apocryphal) story of the First World War, the message was passed along the line: 'Send reinforcements, we're going to advance.' By the time the message reached its final intended recipient it had become: 'Send three-and-fourpence, we're going to a dance.'

Three-and-fourpence was the equivalent of 17p in pre-decimal (i.e. pre-1971) UK currency.

In the financial context the chain begins with the individuals who collectively own the available savings. From them the savings flow through a chain of intermediaries until they reach their final destination – the companies and other organisations which employ society's savings in their day-to-day operations. And the chain does not stop there; once the financial resources have passed through the *external* market into an organisation, they then flow down *internally* through divisions and departments until they reach the commercial equivalent of the military front line. At every stage, the investor or intermediary or manager providing the financial resources may – or should – seek to determine how the funds will be used, and to put in place reporting mechanisms to establish whether and to what extent those objectives have been achieved.

But there is one crucial difference between the financial and the military chains of command. The financial chain is in a very important sense not a line but a circle. The financial equivalent of the lowly foot-soldier is not only responsible for the ultimate deployment of financial resources at the battle-front; he or she is also – through his or her pension rights or life insurance policies – the ultimate provider of those resources and therefore the ultimate giver of orders.

It is appropriate to end the course with a detailed study of control mechanisms because this process of control brings together the two main strands in this course – accounting and finance. As we saw in Unit 1, the purpose of financial accounts is to give an historical account of how managers have exercised the stewardship of the resources entrusted to them. It therefore seemed natural to express targets and objectives in the same language of accounting. However, the developing study of finance theory has shown that the conventions of financial accounting offer at best an imperfect, and at worst a positively misleading, insight into how well the managers of a business are fulfilling their objective. In the case of a commercial enterprise, an objective may be to maximise shareholder wealth and, in the case of a not-for-profit organisation, it may be to achieve maximum value for money.

So, a variety of financial criteria have been, and continue to be, developed both to capture more accurately the overriding objectives of the providers of finance and to measure the performance of the users. These criteria vary from management accounting (a form of accounting used internally by organisations to reflect the commercial realities of their activities more accurately or more appropriately than is permitted by the artificial straitjacket of external or financial accounting regulations) to a range of more sophisticated performance measures. One of the best known of these is **economic value added**, or EVA for short. EVA is a registered trademark of a US firm, Stern Stewart, and is a measure for determining to what extent an organisation (and each operating entity within it) has added or destroyed value during a given period, after making appropriate allowance for the return necessary to compensate investors for the capital provided.

EVA will be discussed in more detail in Section 3.3 of this unit.

We have to observe a subtle but important distinction between commercial and non-commercial organisations in their use of financial control techniques. We said earlier that, in the case of a commercial enterprise, the overriding duty of management is to maximise the owners' wealth, and in the case of a not-for-profit organisation, it is to achieve maximum value for money. In fact, the divide is less clear-cut than this: value for money may not be the only objective for, say, a public-sector body and wealth maximisation for shareholders of a private-sector company ignores the perhaps implicit objectives relating to stakeholders such as customers and employees.

For example, the ultimate objective of the National Health Service or of the education system or of a public-service broadcaster like the BBC is not financial, but financial considerations do figure very prominently in any assessment of how efficiently the managers are achieving their non-financial objectives. As a result, whereas properly formulated financial

The BBC in its more formal days

criteria are the ultimate yardstick for measuring commercial managers' performance, in a non-commercial context financial criteria are often a proxy, a conveniently 'hard' (but sometimes deceptive in their apparent objectivity) substitute for elusively 'soft' objectives like 'the health of the community'.

Similarly, the purely financial objectives of commercial enterprises may be tempered or qualified by other, parallel, objectives. One example is that of so-called **ethical investment**, i.e. the conscious avoidance of investing in organisations which exploit vulnerable minority groups or animals, or which harm the environment. Pension fund trustees of local authorities and of private-sector firms may place some or all of the funds for which they are responsible in funds, such as the one described in Box 1.2:

BOX 1.2 NPI GLOBAL CARE

'The NPI Global Care investment team's sole activity is the management of socially responsible screened investment funds ...

The NPI Global Care research team identifies companies that are either in 'industries of the future' or 'best in class' with respect to financial, environmental and social aspects. Identifying 'industries of the future' such as pollution abatement, water management, public transport, education and healthcare enables the group to gain a competitive advantage over mainstream fund managers.

In more traditional sectors, such as retail banking and food retailers, the group identifies companies that have high quality management reflected by the company's approach to environmental and social issues.'

Source: NPI Global Care Pensions Portfolio Review

We have already said that in this final unit of the course it is appropriate to draw together the main strands from earlier units. But it is reasonable to suppose that you are also looking to the future and are considering how you might use what you have learned from this course to make better sense – and better use – of your external environment.

Activity 1.1

Before you begin, listen to Audio 5, 'Future trends', in which members of the Course Team attempt to identify some of the key themes of the course which they believe represent the main trends in financial strategy. Which of the future trends identified in the audio will affect you most?

Outline of Unit 10

The unit is entitled 'Internal and External Finance' and we shall follow this distinction in our detailed examination of how finance is used as a practical instrument of control.

First, in Section 2, 'Corporate governance', we shall look at corporate governance issues in the private-sector context, such as how shareholders ensure that a company's managers act in their best interests; what sanctions they can invoke against recalcitrant management. What other constraints and incentives can be brought to bear on company managers?

Is the market for corporate control (effectively, the threat of a hostile take-over) an efficient substitute for truly committed shareholders who work with management rather than vote with their feet – by selling their shares – when managers do not perform to plan? Can we learn useful lessons from the apparently stark contrast between the market-driven culture of the USA and UK and the bank-driven culture of continental Europe, with its emphasis on large, long-term strategic shareholdings?

In Section 3, 'Internal v. external reporting', we turn our attention to the *external* dimensions of financial control in the private sector, with a look at how senior managers adapt to the financial objectives imposed by stakeholders, and the *internal* dimensions of financial control, namely the typical disciplines and procedures with which a well-run company plans and controls its capital and revenue budgets. We shall look at the differences between internal management accounting and external financial reporting, and we shall see that their approaches are complementary rather than contradictory, through the use of such measures as return on capital employed and economic value added. By such means, the techniques of corporate governance, which are used by external investors to keep management in line, can be replicated internally down each stage of the management ladder, to ensure that every level within the organisation is aiming for the same objectives.

Section 4, 'Audit and Accountability in the Public Sector', takes a corresponding look at the external and internal dimensions of financial control and performance measurement in a non-profit-making context. This takes the form of a detailed study of the development of value-for-money criteria for the management and audit of public-sector organisations, and highlights both the similarities and the inevitable differences between the public and private sectors. In particular, it looks at the gradual adoption by the public sector of accruals and resource accounting, in which managers are judged by measures such as return on capital employed and charged a cost of capital for resources used.

The final section, 'Performance measurement and investment', extends the issues of control and performance measurement to the investors themselves, in particular the institutional investors who are the dominant shareholders in the Anglo-Saxon corporate sectors. In this sense, the pension fund manager is herself a link in the chain, and is subject to the continuous scrutiny and assessment of the ultimate investors – represented by pension scheme trustees – seeking to achieve their own financial objectives, that is, to maximise their pension fund returns over time, subject to risk constraints.

Objectives of the unit

You may recall that early on in Unit 1 of this course we staked a bold claim for finance, when we said that it is almost unique among management disciplines because it continuously pervades every level of an organisation's activity. Our overall aim in this final unit of the course is to demonstrate to you, using the techniques which you have learned in the intervening units, how and why this claim is justified in practice.

In particular, we aim to show you:
- the basic principles of financial control which are employed throughout the savings and investment process, from the individual assessing the performance of his pension fund against his long-term

investment objectives, to the departmental manager judging his unit's performance against its operating budget

- the main systems employed by providers of finance and by the markets in order to align the users' behaviour with the providers' investment objectives

- the analogous procedures adopted by the controllers and trustees of public-sector and not-for-profit organisations to ensure that their managers achieve their financial objectives, in particular by maximising value for money.

When you have completed your study of this unit, you should be able to:

- assess the relevance and relative efficiency of different structures of corporate governance

- describe how external investment managers and internal line managers assess the performance of different investments and operating units respectively

- show how performance measures such as economic value added, cash flow return on investment and discounted cash flow analysis can be used both as external and as internal performance measures

- apply the principles of value-for-money auditing in the context of the public sector

- describe the financial objectives and performance measures used by institutional investors such as pension funds.

2 CORPORATE GOVERNANCE

2.1   Market-based systems   **10**

2.2   Relationship-based systems   **14**

Summary   **17**

In this section, we look at corporate governance and compare the two main systems, market-based and relationship-based. We discuss the advantages and disadvantages of each in the context of motivating managers to act in the stakeholders' best interests given the changing trends in corporate ownership.

Corporate governance comprises the systems and structures through which a firm interacts with outsider holders of ownership claims. It includes the processes adopted and developed by boards of directors to exercise the rights delegated to them by outside claimants. Corporate governance can be said to set the organisational 'rules of the game' for top managers and has a critical impact on organisations because it strongly influences the rules of the game for all stakeholders.

In the public sector, stakeholders include customers, taxpayers, voters, creditors, suppliers, bankers, Parliament, government departments, and public bodies. In the private sector, stakeholders include the community at large, customers, employees, the government, regulators, investors, bankers, creditors and suppliers.

A company's ownership and financial structure influence its governance. However, there are a number of types of ownership and governance structures around the world where ownership does not necessarily bring control. This has occurred with the listing of firms on stock markets in order to gain access to finance in the form of debt and equity.

2.1 MARKET-BASED SYSTEMS

In the USA, for example, the separation of ownership and control, first pointed out by Berle and Means (1932), has become even more marked in the late twentieth century. Jensen and Meckling (1976), in their paper which views the firm as a nexus of contracts, argued that, with separation of ownership and control, managers would be unlikely to try to maximise shareholder value, as the text books assumed they would, and concentrate instead on acquiring luxuries such as the executive jet or power through size.

Managers of listed US firms own small percentages of the shares in the companies they manage. Jensen and Murphy, as recently as 1990, stated that the average Chief Executive Officer (CEO) of a listed US firm holds 0.03% of the equity of the company for which he works and receives 5 cents in additional remuneration for every $1,000 added to shareholder value, allowing for bonus schemes and share options as well as straight shareholdings. Murphy (1985) reported that CEO remuneration was in fact three times more sensitive to size (measured by total assets or sales) than shareholder value.

So, who does own these firms? In the USA, the major owners are individual investors, followed by investing institutions which hold over 40% of shares in listed companies. In the UK, the importance of investing institutions is even more marked as they control over two thirds of all shares listed on the UK stock market, with individual investors directly holding less than 20%. Investing institutions consist of pension funds, insurance companies and mutual funds. The rapid growth of funded pension schemes and tax-relief-assisted savings policies linked to insurance has meant that the investing institutions globally now control hundreds of billions of dollars worth of investments. The greater importance of the individual investor in the USA is also partly linked to pensions – individuals can set up their own pension plans to invest in equities and still gain tax relief. In the UK, the tax relief tends to be linked to investment via an intermediary – the investing institution.

However, one common characteristic of these individual and institutional holdings is that no single investor or institution holds a dominant shareholding. For individuals, the reason for their lack of importance is clear – few individuals are rich enough to make an impact in terms of percentage shareholding. But investing institutions, such as pension funds and insurance companies, have substantial sums at their disposal and could, if they so wished, acquire control of, or at least influence, the companies in which they invest. The main reason why they do not (Jensen, 1991) is to do with regulation. In the USA, the regulation comes from the Glass Steagall Act implemented in the 1930s to combat fraud such as banks issuing worthless shares – for a fee – and then putting them straight into their clients' investment portfolios. In the UK, in order to protect the ultimate beneficiaries, most pension funds are required to diversify their investments and are prevented from putting, say, 10% of their funds in any one company. This requirement not to put all the 'equity eggs' in one basket has led to pension funds holding equity portfolios with 60 or more different shares in each, leaving them without the time or resources to monitor each company's senior management effectively. Indeed, as we shall see in Section 5, some institutional investors believe that it is not their job to interfere in management. They feel that they do not have managerial expertise and that they would lose their independent attitude to investment by getting closer to the management, and this – showing perhaps as reluctance to sell the shares of a poorly performing company – could well lead to under-performance on their part, causing the beneficiaries or their representatives to complain.

The diffuse ownership structure of listed companies under the so-called market-based system of corporate governance has meant that managers of these firms have had a relatively free hand to adopt the management systems, strategies and remuneration structures they desire. The voting rights of shareholders, whilst real, are in the vast majority of cases not pooled against management in any organised fashion. Even if they are, the giving of proxy votes to management (as many investing institutions do) means that any incipient shareholder rebellion can easily be quashed.

> At present, when the US institutions become dissatisfied with management, they have few options other than to sell their shares. Moreover, managers' complaints about the churning of financial institutions' portfolios ring hollow: most prefer churning to a system in which those institutions would actually have direct power to correct a management problem. Few CEOs today like the idea of having institutions with substantial stock ownership sitting on their corporate board. That would bring about the monitoring of managerial activities by people who bear part of the wealth consequences of managerial mistakes and who are not beholden to the CEO for their directorships.
>
> *(Jensen, 1991, p. 21)*

However, even in an equity-oriented country such as the UK, small, family-based firms are still in the majority. There are over 2,500 companies listed on the UK stock market out of a total population of around 500,000 firms (Franks and Mayer, 1997). But large, listed companies dominate the economy. Almost 80% of the largest 700 companies are listed and the market value of listed companies in the UK is equivalent to around 80% of total GDP.

The directors' rail service?

In the market-based system, corporate control through appropriate corporate governance systems is supposed to make sure that management acts in the best interests of shareholders. There are a number of ways in which this can be implemented. First, executives can be paid in such a way as to align their own and shareholders' financial objectives. We will see in the next section how performance measures linked to shareholder value are being introduced on a fairly wide scale. Second, there can be control imposed by non-executive directors who act as representatives of external shareholders on the board. However, as the extract from Jensen suggests, many non-executive directors are friends rather than potential critics of the CEO.

The third corporate control approach is known as the **market for corporate control**. In other words, if management does not act in the shareholders' best interests, shareholders can vote more effectively with their feet than their pens and sell their shares in the market-place. If enough investors do so, this will eventually force the share price down, making the company vulnerable to hostile take-over. Although the evidence for 'disciplinary' take-overs is not conclusive, there is some support for a link between the market for corporate control and the correction of managerial failure. For example, in a UK study, Franks and Mayer (1997) cite evidence of considerable restructuring after take-overs. They found that levels of asset disposals and restructurings were significantly higher in cases where bids were either hostile or followed managerial control changes. There is also evidence that executive directors either resign or lose their jobs after successful hostile bids (nearly 80% in the Franks and Mayer study), although there is also evidence that hostile bids are only a limited form of corporate control, since they cause acquirers to incur large transaction costs and to pay a premium over the market share price for control (see, for example, Bradley *et al.*, 1988).

However, creditors can also have a role to play without the need for a hostile take-over. Gilson and Vetsuypens (1993) find that, for 77 US firms that suffered financial distress, almost one third of CEOs were replaced and those who remained suffered pay and bonus reductions. Under the market-based system prevalent in the USA and the UK, it is the directors, the institutional investors and the creditors who are the dominant stakeholders in the organisation.

We have seen that, when performance is weak, and managers do not change organisational structures to improve performance, the market for corporate control can force changes in financial policy that induce organisational change. The traditional way to do this was either to get the banks in or to create a situation where a hostile bid was inevitable. Existing managers were fired and new managers put in. However, what has become more common in recent years is the use of financial structure to force management change.

There are a number of ways in which this can be done. The closest to the hostile take-over is the leveraged management buyout in which managers are given or buy significant equity stakes in the business they manage and external investors such as debt and equity providers are involved in the strategic and internal management decisions. The aim of the management buyout is clear – to realign more closely ownership and control.

The early leveraged buyouts (or LBOs) were ways of streamlining unprofitable conglomerates or of paying out excess cash in organisations which had reached a mature stage in the product cycle. Later LBOs were done without hostile take-overs, by restructuring the finance of the organisation without the need for a change in management. In such cases as these, directors could use the change in financial structure – which usually increased bankruptcy risk – as a whip to force managers lower down the hierarchy to cut costs, sell off unwanted assets and manage cash flow more effectively. Performance measures which ensure that junior managers achieve the objectives set by the board, such as the value-based measures we shall discuss in Section 3, become more crucial in organisations in which there is no slack.

Management buyouts (MBOs) were another means of changing performance through ownership. Divisions of large organisations were often run at less than optimal performance through the need to compete with other divisions for funds or the need to subsidise poorly performing parts of the business. By switching ownership, new organisational and management processes could be put in place which improved performance.

In the public sector, the same ideas have been applied, with independently managed public separate entities (**quangos**) now run on private company lines, with tight financial performance measures used to manage organisations previously managed purely on non-financial or easily achievable targets. Section 4 describes these changes in public-sector corporate governance strategies in more detail.

2.2 RELATIONSHIP-BASED SYSTEMS

The alternative relationship-based, or bank-based, system of corporate governance is found in countries such as Germany, Japan and France. In these countries, ownership is concentrated among a number of corporate or banking shareholders rather than diffused as in the Anglo-American model, stock markets are relatively illiquid, and hostile take-overs very difficult to implement. For example, in Germany, there are fewer than 700 quoted companies and in France fewer than 500. In France and Germany, the value of quoted companies amounts to less than 25% of GDP and, in both countries, over 80% of these companies have a shareholder holding more than 25% of the shares (Franks and Mayer, 1997).

Control is exercised through long-term relationships between managers and banks and corporate shareholders. They may be formal, as in the case of Germany where bank representatives and employees sit on supervisory boards to which the board of directors reports. They may also be informal, as in the Japanese case where outside directors with relationships to creditor banks, say, are only appointed when there is evidence of deteriorating performance (Kaplan, 1997).

Table 2.1 A comparison of German, Japanese and US governance systems			
	Germany	**Japan**	**USA**
Executive compensation	Moderate	Low	High
Board of directors	Management/ supervisory	Primarily insiders	Primarily outsiders
Ownership	Concentrated; high family/ corporate/bank	Less concentrated; high bank/high corporate/low management	Diffuse/non-corporate
Capital markets	Relatively illiquid	Somewhat liquid	Very liquid
Take-over/ control market	Minor	Minor	Major
Banking system	Universal banking	Main bank system	Fragmented

Source: Kaplan, 1997

Monitoring is the main form of corporate governance which takes place in the relationship-based system of corporate governance. In Germany, Japan and France, executive remuneration schemes closely linked to share price performance are rare. Hostile take-overs are also rare. For example, in Germany, the total number of mergers was one-half of that in the UK during the 1980s. Moreover, there have been just four recorded cases of hostile take-overs in Germany since World War II and three of those four occurred in the 1990s (Franks and Mayer, 1997). Similar statistics exist for Japan and France.

Possible explanations for the lack of a market for corporate control include the dominant role of the banks as stakeholders. In many companies they are the major shareholder (both directly and indirectly as proxy holders of votes for individuals with shares lodged with the banks) and also have close relationships with the management either through membership of the supervisory board or more informally. In such cases, no hostile bids could succeed without the consent of the banks who traditionally prefer to implement change themselves if they believe it is needed rather than have it foisted on the company from the outside.

Another explanation for the failure in the market for corporate control is the existence of limitations on shareholder voting rights, whatever the size of the holding. In some companies, in Germany for example, the voting rights of any one shareholder can be limited by shareholder resolution to, say, 10 or 15% of the total votes, regardless of the size of the shareholding. So, building up a sizeable stake in a German company does not necessarily bring with it the control required to implement change.

The illiquidity of stock markets and the traditional strong role of banks in France, Germany and Japan have limited access to equity funding for the larger companies in these countries. As companies have felt the need to grow in order to succeed in global markets and as governments have felt the need to privatise large utilities, so the capital markets have begun to increase in importance and a shift towards the market-based system of corporate governance has begun. Companies have begun to pay lip service to *shareholder value* rather than the previous emphasis on *stakeholder* – particularly banks, fellow corporates and employees – *value*.

However, for there to be a switch to the market-based systems of the UK and the USA, there would have to be an increase in the number and/or size of investing institutions. It is demand from both individuals and intermediaries for equities which are liquid, long-term, and offer positive real rates of return which have maintained the capital markets in these countries. Only if governments encourage equity saving over debt, say by allowing a market for corporate control to develop and by encouraging a move to funded pension schemes rather than the current 'pay as you go' systems, will the shift to a market-based system of corporate governance evolve. Monitoring through investor-focused accounts and share price movements will then replace monitoring through supervisory boards.

Pay as you go pension systems are those where today's pensions are paid out of current contributions rather than paid out of the previous contributions of the individuals concerned.

There has been much discussion on whether the market-based system or relationship-based corporate governance system is to be preferred. The market-based Anglo-American system would appear superior in terms of achieving the objective of maximising shareholder value. The system is apparently best achieved by an active market in corporate control, which removes inefficiencies such as underperforming conglomerates and excess free cash flow. It may be, however, that too much emphasis on maximisation of shareholder wealth ignores the needs of other stakeholders such as employees, although proponents of the market-based system disagree:

Value-maximising does not mean that stockholders are an especially deserving group, or that corporate stakeholders other than stockholders should be ignored in management's decision-making. Maximising value, in fact, means allocating corporate resources (to the point where marginal costs equal marginal benefits) among all groups or interests that affect firm value. Value maximising decision-making devotes resources to members of each important corporate constituency to improve the terms on which they contract with the company, to maintain the firm's reputation, and to reduce the threat of restrictive regulation. In this sense, there is no conflict between management's service to its stockholders and to other corporate stakeholders.

(Jensen, 1991, p. 21)

Exercise 2.1

The following four extracts from Annual Reports highlight differing corporate objectives for firms which are all discussed in B821 *Financial Strategy*. These firms are: BP, an oil multinational; Daimler-Benz, a German vehicle manufacturer; Boots, a UK chemists chain; and Scott Bader, a chemicals company owned in trust for the benefit of its employees. Which statement belongs to which company?

A   'Our objective is to maximise the value of the company for the benefit of its shareholders. We will do so by investing in our businesses to generate strong cash flows and superior long-term returns.

Whilst vigorously pursuing our commercial interests, we will, at all times, seek to enhance our reputation as a well managed, ethical and socially responsible company.'

B   'Our mission is to build and sustain our international enterprise through benefits to our customers, demonstrating the value of our way through quality, service and innovation.'

C   'Your Board is committed to the best principles of corporate governance. For you, the shareholders, our commitment is to building not just short-term but long-term value.

Company C's Board of directors is responsible for understanding the requirements of shareholders and the political, environmental and social environment in which the group operates.'

D   'The road to our former earning power brings with it the loss of jobs and considerable costs for the company. But it is simultaneously the road to social responsibility ... by focussing Company D on profitable core businesses, we have chosen the road to a successful future.'

Critics of the alternative relationship-based model, such as Demsetz and Lehn (1985), also argue that, given the concentrated ownership characteristic of this type of corporate governance model:

• managers and others are forced to bear specific risk which could better be borne by investors who are fully diversified; and

• concentrated ownership allows insiders to capture private benefits and thus penalises those outside shareholders who do invest.

However, a major criticism of the market-based system, put forward by authors such as Hutton (1995), is the short-term approach which it engenders in management.

Activity 2.2

Read the article by Hutton entitled 'Stakeholder capitalism' in the Course Reader. Are you convinced by his arguments? Which corporate governance model best suits the needs of the organisation of the twenty-first century?

SUMMARY

In this section, we have looked at what is meant by corporate governance, that is the systems and structures through which a firm interacts with outside holders of ownership claims. We first examined the market-based system which is prevalent in the UK and USA and which views the shareholder as the dominant stakeholder in the firm. Changes over time in corporate governance structures under this system have been due to the separation between ownership and control in firms based in these countries. The relationship-based system of corporate governance is the model adopted in countries such as France, Germany and Japan where the capital markets and hence shareholders have typically had less influence. Here employees and lenders have had a higher role in the governance process. However, as these countries' stock markets become more important in the provision of capital to firms, so there is pressure for moves towards the market-based system.

3 INTERNAL V. EXTERNAL REPORTING

3.1   Management and financial accounting   **18**

3.2   Trends in performance measurement   **21**

3.3   Economic and accounting performance measures   **25**

        Summary   **39**

In this section we look at how internal and external reporting for the organisation are changing over time and becoming more integrated. More commonly known as management accounting and financial accounting, these functions have historically been segregated, with separate professional bodies and separate career structures. However, in recent years, the traditional barriers have begun to break down as pressure for performance and added value have increasingly forced organisations to make sure that internal and external financial goals are congruent.

We show how the trend has been away from control of inputs such as cash for investment towards control through measurement of performance relative to targeted outcomes such as share returns. Such targets are now being driven by outside investors and imposed on senior managers and these in turn are defining equivalent targets for divisional managers. We will describe in this section how value-added measures, in particular economic value added (EVA), are taking precedence over traditional accounting measures of performance such as earnings per share or divisional profit. An equivalent change is taking place in the public sector, with value-added measures being implemented in a number of countries around the world as governments attempt not to maximise shareholder value but to minimise costs and spread public-sector spending more thinly. Section 4, 'Public-sector financial management', will explore performance measurement in more detail.

3.1 MANAGEMENT AND FINANCIAL ACCOUNTING

We saw in Unit 1 how the focus of the management accounting function is internal, whereas the financial accounting function is external, hence their names. Management accounts, produced for internal consumption, have three main uses:

For this reason, management accounting is also called 'internal reporting' and financial accounting called 'external reporting'.

- planning
- decision-making
- control.

A core element of management accounting is the budgeting process in which budgets are prepared for a number of future periods, and this allows planning of such issues as how much working capital and what inventory levels will be needed in the future. The second main use of management accounts is to contribute to the decision-making process. For example, information provided by management accountants forms a crucial part of any capital expenditure proposal. For both planning and decision-making purposes, therefore, management accounting information often has the characteristic of being forward-looking, with forecasts of future outcomes a major aspect of any management accountant's job. However, the third main use of management accounts is control of operations through the measurement of performance of middle or divisional managers by senior managers: as encouragement to achieve the desired outcomes, divisional managers are incentivised through the setting of appropriate performance benchmarks. As further encouragement, performance relative to these benchmarks may also influence pay and bonuses. Thus, performance measurement is a major strand in management accounting and accounting measures such as target profit before tax have commonly been used.

Turning to financial accounting, or external reporting, this also has three main functions:

- decision-making
- stewardship
- accountability.

The decision-making function of financial accounts has an exact parallel in management accounts. However, unlike management accounts, financial accounts are not used for senior management decision-making, rather for the decision-making needs of the stakeholders of the organisation. Over the years, there has been much discussion as to which interest groups or stakeholders are interested in financial accounts. For example, the increased publication of **social accounts** recognises that the community in which an organisation operates, its employees and customers, all have an interest in its activities and need certain information, such as on health and safety, to make decisions. More traditionally, the Continental European model of accounting requires financial accounts to be produced in order to allow governments to determine the tax liability of each organisation. For the privatised utilities, regulators have an interest in studying published accounts to check profitability, asset values, financial structure and prices charged to the customer.

However, particularly under the Anglo-Saxon model of accounting, it has been recognised that the primary user of accounts is the investor, particularly the equity investor, and the decision that they wish to make on the basis of the financial accounts is that of whether to sell, hold or buy shares.

Each stakeholder will want to see different numbers in financial accounts and managers may wish to present data in a different way for each stakeholder. For example, managers will wish to show low taxable profits if tax collectors or regulators are studying the accounts and high taxable profits if the accounts are primarily aimed at investors. Social accounts are produced by organisations which report on social issues of interest to stakeholders such as employees, consumers and members of the local community.

> A shareholder has to make a decision whether to sell, hold or buy the company's shares and the information in the report and accounts should be designed to assist in that decision and that is the sole purpose of the report and accounts.
>
> *(Chisman, 1998, p. 17)*

The stewardship function of financial accounts is equivalent to the control function of management accounts and is designed to check that the stewards of the organisation (directors in the case of a firm) have acted in the best interests of the owners, or shareholders. This requirement has influenced the historic cost nature of accounts (how much did directors actually spend?) as well as the requirement for financial accounts to be audited by third parties, in case directors falsified the accounts. So, shareholders can use financial accounts to check that the managers entrusted with their funds have not embezzled funds, and have acted in their best interests. In the case of public-sector accounts, say for quangos such as NHS trusts, accounts perform a similar function, with owners in this case replaced by taxpayers.

However, we saw in Section 2 that there has been a separation of management and ownership in the modern firm, particularly in the USA and the UK, with managers owning relatively small percentages of equity and having objectives which may be different from those of the shareholders. Financial accounts have proved to have a limited role in making managers 'accountable', partly because financial accounts are backward looking, appearing months or even years after the events to which they refer: and partly because accounting rules permit the omission of certain information of relevance to the owners and also the leading or lagging of other data to show a perhaps misleading picture of true profitability.

Activity 3.1

 For the extent of possible variations in profit due to choosing different accounting policies, see the extract from the 1992 Queens Moat Annual Report and Accounts in the Measuring Performance section of the Course Reader (Case Study 8).

This separation of ownership and management of companies has led to attempts to reintroduce congruence between management and investor objectives through executive compensation rather than merely the publishing of financial accounts. The key figure in a set of financial accounts was traditionally earnings per share and senior managers attempted to manage this figure to their advantage, often taking decisions which enhanced earnings per share but which did not necessarily enhance the owners' wealth, that is, shareholder value. Increasing awareness of this problem, brought to light when some firms suffered during the recession of the early 1990s despite having reported glowing results in their financial accounts, has led to a trend to encourage senior management to act more directly in shareholders' interests via financial incentives rather than control. There has been an increase in executive pay linked to total performance measures of shareholder return or share price performance relative to an index, and in share option schemes, where option values are linked to share price. This can clearly be seen by reading a set of UK or US Annual Reports and Accounts and studying the detailed information now available on executive pay.

BOOTS, REMUNERATION COMMITTEE'S REPORT, ANNUAL REPORT AND ACCOUNTS FOR THE YEAR ENDED 31 MARCH, 1997

Share ownership provides an effective way to align the interests of shareholders and executives. Therefore, half of an executive director's long term bonus is payable in shares of the company.

However, such shareholder value-based performance measures for senior managers differ from the accounting-based measures traditionally used to measure divisional manager performance and this has led to differences between divisional and senior management objectives within the same organisation (O'Hanlon and Peasnell, 1998, p. 3). In the late 1990s, consultants began to grapple with this problem by recommending that the same performance measures and incentive schemes used externally for senior managers be used internally for divisional managers. In fact, the measures they suggest are a compromise between the traditional accounting-based measures used by management accountants and the economic value-based measures of relevance to shareholders.

In the remainder of this section, we examine in more detail the relationship between management and financial accounts in the context of performance measures. We show how internal and external performance and incentive measures are becoming more connected through the abandonment of the traditional top-down earnings per share model of management and replaced by performance measures such as EVA which reflect changes in shareholder value estimated from accounting data. These are designed to ensure that internal management actions achieve the desired objective at the stakeholder level, without the veil of accounting causing inappropriate actions.

3.2 TRENDS IN PERFORMANCE MEASUREMENT

The main ingredient in any management control system is measurement. Measurement of operations, processes and organisational components of an enterprise requires the responsibility for outcomes to be assigned and accepted. The measure or measurements metrics must be chosen consistent with top management's objectives for the organisation. They must be perceived to be fair. The variables included in the measure must be well-defined, and the measures must inform management of what action should be taken and when to take it

(Dillon and Owers, 1997, p. 36)

The above statement gives the requirements for the ideal performance measure or **metric** to be used internally within an organisation. It assumes that top management's objectives are the appropriate objectives for the company – in other words, that senior managers are choosing objectives which are designed to enhance shareholder value.

As already mentioned, it was not always thus. The traditional model of the 1960s was that of senior executives fixated on growth in earnings per share and this objective was translated into given profit targets for the individual divisions. Since capital spending was tightly controlled at the top, through some form of capital rationing, this meant that new share issues were infrequent, so that any increase in profits fed through to increases in earnings per share rather than diluting them. The diversification boom of the 1960s and 1970s, when conglomerates such as Trafalgar House and Hanson were created, allowed further enhancement of earnings through the acquisition of low PE firms.

See Unit 6, Section 5.3 for an example of how to enhance earnings per share through acquisition, an activity known as 'bootstrapping'.

In addition, diversification reduced earnings volatility, allowing senior managers to deliver what they had promised – steady growth. This, as we shall see, did not necessarily translate into increased share prices on the stock market, but commentators such as Donaldson (1961) argued that senior managers at that time were more concerned with a broader set of stakeholders, which included employees, suppliers and lenders as well as shareholders, and so were neither explicitly nor implicitly attempting to maximise shareholder wealth.

Whatever happened to corporate planners?

At the divisional level, the annual ritual of divisional budget targets encouraged divisional managers to underestimate the profits their divisions would make in order to do well relative to their performance benchmarks and hence boost their own bonuses. They could do this since they knew better than the head office corporate planners what their profit potential was and so were able to create what were in effect hidden reserves which they could bring out when the bad times came. This satisficing behaviour on the part of divisional managers was not consistent with the senior managers' maximisation of the earnings per share objective, still less with the shareholders' objective of maximising shareholder value. Divisional managers' objectives became the achievement of moderate growth in profits through efficiency gains or through the acquisition of additional assets from which to generate more profits.

By the 1980s, the conglomerates which had been the darlings of the stock market were underperforming in terms of shareholder returns. This led to hostile take-over bids and corporate restructurings, in particular in the form of leveraged buyouts. These restructurings essentially made money out of the fact that earnings are not the same as cash flow and that value is more closely linked to the latter than to the former. By targeting firms which had apparently low earnings and hence appeared expensive on a PE measure but which had high cash flow and hence low price to cash flow multiples, hostile raiders were able to make considerable profits.

BOX 3.1   DR PEPPER

In the early 1980s, Dr. Pepper, a US firm producing canned fizzy drinks, similar to Coca Cola, had fallen on hard times. Earnings had fallen for the first time in years and the share price was trading at $17 compared with an all-time high of $24. A management buyout bid at $22 was successful and management were later able to sell out for a rate of return of several hundred percent on their investment. Their key insight had been to recognise that earnings were artificially low due to major investment in regional bottling plants in recent years. The depreciation charge on these investments was high, causing earnings to be reduced. However, not only was capital expenditure not required for several years to come, there was also an opportunity to sell some of the bottling plants for cash and to squeeze net operating assets through more effective inventory management. This meant that cash flow for Dr Pepper was far higher than earnings suggested, although the PE multiple of 23.7 on a bid price of $22 made the shares seem expensive. As management realised, Dr Pepper was cheap on a price to cash flow basis and they profited from the fact that the stock market was not yet aware of this.

Investors began to appreciate that earnings growth was not a sufficient condition for share price growth and that the figures in the income statement did not always correlate with shareholder value. Neither did the balance sheet help predict share values. Given the historic nature of the asset values, investors gradually became aware that book values underestimated property values (in the 1970s), brand values (in the 1980s), net pension fund asset values (in the 1980s) and intellectual property values (in the 1990s). There was a growing gap between what financial accounts showed and what the stock market believed. The catalyst was what we described in Section 2 as the market for corporate control. As the take-over boom of the 1980s accelerated, even analysts were caught napping. The large premium of offer price to current share price in many bids revealed that potential acquirers were valuing their targets more highly using price to cash flow and EV to EBITDA multiples than were the stock market analysts, still valuing shares on a PE basis.

As well as using simple price to cash flow multiples, bidders were valuing firms using discounted cash flow techniques. This required an analysis of the cost of capital and LBOs showed that it was not just the operating cash flows but also the cost of capital required to fund the investment which could affect share value. Value could be added by financing with a low WACC as well as from managing operations more efficiently or achieving sales growth. The cost of capital had become a key value driver.

See Unit 4 if you need to revise WACC.

The wave of LBOs did not alone trigger the change in attitude towards valuation and the importance of different accounting and finance numbers. What also did was the fall in share price of companies such as General Mills in the US and later Hanson in the UK. Investors began to look at what drove share performance and argued that earnings, although an indicator, did not tell the whole story. First of all, cash flow was a better predictor of share value than earnings, quite simply because, as we have seen in Units 4 and 6, the present value of an entity is the present value of the expected future cash flows. Second, investors became aware that, as capital was costly, companies which were able to invest at more than the WACC would surely add value for shareholders whereas companies which wasted capital, and did not earn enough to compensate investors, given the risk, were destroying shareholder value. By the 1990s, a number of companies had built up cash surpluses and they were using these to make investments which, although they increased earnings per share in the absolute sense, and added growth, were negative in terms of net present value once the cost of capital used was taken into account. Investors began to realise that, in an increasingly competitive world with many industries suffering excess capacity, efficient use of capital resources was more likely to lead to enhanced share value than growth for growth's sake.

Activity 3.2

Read the comments in Box 3.2 overleaf and try to think of companies or organisations which you have come across which you feel still have excess capital or are not achieving sufficient returns on capital employed to ensure their survival in the longer term. Do you think that setting appropriate performance measures would be sufficient to improve the situation or will the 'market for corporate control' solution be required?

BOX 3.2   THE TYRE INDUSTRY

'The solution to excess capacity in the tire industry came about through the market for corporate control. Every major U.S. tire firm was either taken over or restructured in the 1980s. In total, 37 tire plants were shut down in the period 1977–87, and total employment in the industry fell by over 40%.

Capital market and corporate control transactions such as the repurchase of stock (or the purchase of another company) for cash or debt accompanies exit of resources in a very direct way. When Chevron acquired Gulf for $13.2 billion in cash and debt in 1984, the net assets devoted to the oil industry fell by $13.2 billion as soon as the checks were mailed out. In the 1980s, the oil industry had to shrink to accommodate the reduction in the quantity of oil demanded and the reduced rate of growth of demand. This meant paying out to shareholders its huge cash inflows, reducing exploration and development expenditures to bring reserves in line with reduced demands, and closing refining and distribution facilities. Leveraged acquisitions and equity repurchases helped accomplish this for virtually all major U.S. oil firms.

Exit also resulted when KKR acquired RJR-Nabisco for $25 billion in cash and debt in its 1986 leveraged buyout. The tobacco industry must shrink, given the change in smoking habits in response to consumer awareness of cancer threats, and the payout of RJR's cash accomplished this to some extent. RJR's LBO debt also prevented the company from continuing to squander its cash flows on wasteful projects it had planned to undertake prior to the buyout. Thus the buyout laid the groundwork for the efficient reduction of capacity and resources by one of the major firms in the industry.'

M. Jensen, 'The Modern Industrial Revolution, Exit, and the Failure of Internal Control Systems' p. 30.

This phenomenon has not been limited to the USA.

'The Nomura Research Institute published a report (on Japan) which came to the following major conclusions:

- First, the decline in corporate earnings and share prices have by far exceeded those that would have been expected in a purely 'cyclical' downturn, and NRI has attributed the severity of such declines to a 'structural' overcapacity stemming from lax investment criteria employed by Japanese companies.

- Second, the practice of cross-holdings of shares among Japanese firms has prevented shareholders from exerting sufficient influence on management, with negative consequences for efficiency.

- Third, in addition to denying shareholders any means of effective oversight or control over their investment policies, Japanese companies also tend to compound the problem by retaining excess capital rather than returning it to shareholders in the form of higher dividends or share repurchases. Failure to pay out excess capital leads to inefficiency.'

Jochi Aoi, Chairman of the Board, Toshiba Corporation, in 'To Whom does the Company Belong?: A New Management Mission for the Information Age' p. 245.

Source: Chew, 1997

3.3 ECONOMIC AND ACCOUNTING PERFORMANCE MEASURES

In this sub-section, we look at how performance measures have been introduced into organisations, within both external and internal accounting processes, in an attempt to ensure appropriate behaviour on behalf of management. We have seen how the market for corporate control, provided the regulatory framework allows it, is the ultimate means of ensuring that managers act on behalf of shareholders. However, the 1990s have seen a rapid growth in performance measures and related management incentive schemes, which attempt to do this internally rather than waiting for market forces to operate.

The two key characteristics of this new generation of performance measures are that they are related to shareholder value rather than accounting numbers and that they look at returns *after* allowing for the returns expected by investors rather than before. In order to do this they are based on the concept of **economic income** rather than accounting profit, where economic income can be defined as income generated by the company *net* of investors' required returns on capital invested.

Accountants became interested in the concept of economic as opposed to accounting income as far back as the 1930s (Preinreich, 1938). Accounting earnings can be shown to be related to cash flow and hence to economic income in a straightforward manner (Ohlson, 1989, 1995) provided one assumes profits are determined according to what is known as the **comprehensive income** or **clean surplus** basis. To conform to this basis, profits must include all changes in book value during the period (transactions with owners, such as dividend payments, excepted).

If this is the case, we can write:

$$\text{NOPAT}_t = C_t + (A_t - A_{t-1}) \tag{1}$$

Where

$\text{NOPAT}_t = $ Accounting profit for period t

$C_t = $ Cash paid to (net of contributions by) owners for period t where owners are deemed to be all providers of long-term capital, i.e. shareholders and lenders

$A_t = $ Accounting book value of assets at time t

Economic income (also known as **residual income**) is accounting profit adjusted for a charge on capital and can be written:

$$E_t = \text{NOPAT}_t - \text{WACC} \times A_{t-1} \tag{2}$$

where

$E_t = $ Economic income

and

WACC = Weighted average cost of capital, assumed to be constant over time

We know from Unit 6 that the value of an entity such as a firm is the present value of the cash flows to the providers of capital.

So,

$$V_t = \sum_{n=1}^{\infty} \frac{C_{t+n}}{(1+\text{WACC})^n} \qquad (3)$$

where

V_t = Value of company at time t

Substituting for C_t in equation (3) using equations (1) and (2) gives:

$$V_t = \sum_{n=1}^{\infty} \frac{E_{t+n} + (1+\text{WACC})A_{t+n-1} - A_{t+n}}{(1+\text{WACC})^n} \qquad (4)$$

$$= \sum_{n=1}^{\infty} \frac{E_{t+n}}{(1+\text{WACC})^n} + \sum_{n=1}^{\infty} \frac{(1+\text{WACC})A_{t+n-1} - A_{t+n}}{(1+\text{WACC})^n}$$

$$= \sum_{n=1}^{\infty} \frac{E_{t+n}}{(1+\text{WACC})^n}$$

$$+ \frac{(1+\text{WACC})A_t}{(1+\text{WACC})} - \frac{A_{t+1}}{(1+\text{WACC})} + \frac{(1+\text{WACC})A_{t+1}}{(1+\text{WACC})^2}$$

$$- \frac{A_{t+2}}{(1+\text{WACC})^2} + \ldots + \frac{(1+\text{WACC})A_{t+n-1}}{(1+\text{WACC})^n} - \frac{A_{t+n}}{(1+\text{WACC})^n}$$

$$= \sum_{n=1}^{\infty} \frac{E_{t+n}}{(1+\text{WACC})^n} + A_t - \frac{A_{t+n}}{(1+\text{WACC})^n}$$

If we assume in equation (4) that $A_{t+n}/(1+\text{WACC})^n \to 0$ as $n \to \infty$, then we obtain:

$$V_t = A_t + \sum_{n=1}^{\infty} \frac{E_{t+n}}{(1+\text{WACC})^n} \qquad (5)$$

Equation (5) states that the value of a firm is its book value (debt and equity capital) plus the present value of future economic or residual income discounted by the WACC. From this, it is clear that if, in any one year, economic income is negative, the value of the firm will be reduced, hence the expression 'destroying value'. If economic income is positive, the management can be said to have 'added value'.

The attraction of equation (5) is that it allows the value of a company to be expressed as the present value of future income but, instead of cash flows, uses two accounting measures, book value and NOPAT. So, provided accounting policy puts all changes in book value through the income statement, this formula will give the same answer for company value as discounting cash flows would have done in Unit 6.

Accounting income focuses on income available for payment to investors, for example, in the case of NOPAT, the income after tax available to pay interest and dividends. Economic income, as defined in equation (2), focuses on income which can be distributed by an entity to all its owners *after* they have been provided with benchmark returns on the capital they entrusted to the company at the beginning of the period. The benchmark return required by investors is, as we discussed in Unit 4, the weighted average cost of capital. As far as economic income is concerned, the WACC is deemed to be a cost rather than a return. Economic income measures the return available for all owners of capital after allowing for the return they require given the risks they have taken. Economic income is an equivalent concept to *net* present value – both are measures of what is sometimes termed **excess return**.

Economic income in external reporting

At present, financial accounts provide only limited information on economic income. For example, the weighed average cost of capital is not automatically disclosed in the financial accounts and no accounting jurisdiction requires pure clean surplus accounting. However, the UK Accounting Standards Board has been at the head of a move which may spread to other countries (given the influence the UK has within the IASC) towards reporting economic values and economic income measures in financial accounts.

Boots, in the forefront of the UK trend towards shareholder value, supports the Accounting Standards Board in its aims:

FINANCIAL REVIEW, BOOTS PLC, ANNUAL REPORT AND ACCOUNTS FOR THE YEAR ENDED 31 MARCH, 1997

The company fully supports the objectives of the Accounting Standards Board (ASB) in its aim to improve the quality and consistency of financial statements. Over the past twelve months we have commented on ASB pronouncements relevant to our business and we will continue to do so in the future. We are concerned where International Standards depart significantly from UK practice and support the ASB in trying to influence proposed changes in major issues affecting UK practice.

Recognising how difficult it would be to change the measurement of profit in the traditional profit and loss account, UK accounting regulators have introduced the requirement for a new financial income statement. This statement, called the Statement of Total Recognised Gains and Losses (STRGL, pronounced 'struggle'!), attempts to measure clean surplus profit by adding to the profit attributable to shareholders all changes in profit which have been put through the balance sheet rather than the income statement and excluding payments to and from owners. As well as moving towards economic measures of income, the ASB is also attempting to encourage firms to move towards economic values rather than historic cost values in the balance sheet. An increasing number of balance sheet items are, or will be, required to be expressed in terms of measures such as current value or what is known as **value in use** (which requires discounted cash flow forecasts). Taken to its logical conclusion, changes in book value, if assets and liabilities were valued according to ASB wishes, would represent changes in economic value. In such a case, it would be relatively easy for investors to decide, from the financial accounts, which firms had added value and which had destroyed it.

There is substantial support for such measures from the corporate sector, as outlined in Box 3.3 overleaf.

BOX 3.3   LET THE BALANCE SHEET REPORT ON SHAREHOLDER VALUE DIRECTLY

The management role may be thought of as stewardship of shareholder value, or stewardship of the *value* of the company's assets. Historic cost accounts make no attempt to report this so do not measure management's performance of its single most important responsibility. But it does not have to be this way. If the balance sheet is set up to reflect current values of assets it will do the job very nicely of giving a snapshot in time of the performance of that stewardship role. This is what a layman believes the balance sheet says – what the company is worth – its assets at current values minus its liabilities at current values. Essentially, what the management think would be realised from a liquidation or break-up, what they think the company is *worth*. A historic cost balance sheet is meaningless. It has no information content, it is simply the repository of sundry debits and credits. A current value balance sheet is crammed with meaning, and it reports directly upon shareholder value.

And what of profit? Well, the difference between the values at two balance sheet dates, adjusted for any cash flows to or from shareholders, is the total gain in the period and gains can be of several types. It is as yet arguable what are the relative functions of the profit and loss account and the statement of total recognised gains and losses – for example, do you want to differentiate between repeatable and non-repeatable gains, or between gains from trading and gains from holding, or even between historic cost profit and all other gains? However that debate evolves, all you are really doing is reporting the totality of gains in a way which is useful to the user of the accounts. And if the balance sheet is in current values, those gains are gains in shareholder value.

One of the objections to this approach is that managements, and particularly accountants, claim not to be able to estimate the values of assets satisfactorily. We get obfuscation. Examples are quoted with the intent of demonstrating complexity. We get claims that the rules are inoperable and too subjective. Even that it is not the job of management to report upon value – that being the job of the stock market. Tosh. Managements have no difficulty in assessing values when it comes to buying or selling assets or in evaluating mergers and acquisitions. They can forecast revenues to be achieved under very uncertain conditions several years into the future. They can do discounted cash flow analyses. They can estimate their weighted average cost of capital.

No, these arguments will not wash. It is very easy to value businesses because businesses have profit streams. Assets are only components of businesses. Let us not worry about valuing individual assets, this is not where shareholder value lies. Let us estimate the value of the businesses that use the assets. Management has no excuse for not being able to value those.

This principle has already been used by the ASB in several of its standards and exposure drafts. The impairment tests proposed for the valuation of goodwill are entirely what is required. I do not believe that the objectors to the approach gave any indication that this is difficult or impractical to do – merely that they do not want to do it.

So, the portrayal of balance sheets at current values would be a major step forward in allowing shareholders to make their sell, hold or buy decisions.

Managements would be telling the market what they believe the company is worth, what they believe its market capitalisation should be. They would explain how gains or losses in value came about. This, for me, is the balance sheet approach and the right approach – focus on the value shown in the balance sheet and explain the change since last time. Managements who inflate their estimates of values would be punished by the embarrassment of the stock market blowing a raspberry and ascribing a lower market capitalisation. Managements who under-value their assets would be similarly punished by potential under-valuation of their shares and the inconvenience of a take-over bid and losing their jobs. If, in fact, it is the stock market that has it wrong, management can explain how it came to its valuation and invite a re-appraisal. Quite a major step forward.

Of course, managements in many cases would hate this objectivity. It would put their heads on the block. They would have to report directly to shareholders on the value they have created or destroyed – on their own estimates. At first glance this may seem painful or foolhardy, but when you consider that all companies would be doing the same there would be considerable tolerance for a fair degree of inaccuracy, at least at first. As time passed it may be expected that managements and shareholders would become better both at producing current value balance sheets and interpreting them. More importantly, managements would become better at understanding value and creating it.

All of this poses the question of whether these valuations have to be accurate. Of course, one has to concede that they cannot be accurate, but this is no worse than current GAAP under which the book value of real estate is frequently re-estimated. Gains so recorded are noted for what they are and estimates are quite acceptable. The degree of accuracy required is a function of the use to which the information is to be put.

Source: Chisman, 1998

Indeed, some corporates are proposing to provide economic as well as accounting information in their financial accounts without waiting for accounting requirements to change. Carl Wilhelm Ros, chief financial officer of Ericsson, the Swedish mobile telephone company, is reported in *The Economist* as attempting to develop a new method of financial reporting.

Mr Ros hopes to improve on many recent efforts to measure a firm's return over and above its weighted average cost of capital. He has agreed to let Ericsson serve as a test case for Price Waterhouse, which has developed something it calls 'Value Reporting'. Rather than just measuring cash flows internally to guide strategy and compensation, Ericsson will publish the new information, giving investors more detail about how well it is using their capital. It is evidence that the debate among regulators over reporting standards is beginning to be resolved by the companies themselves, acting unilaterally. If Mr Ros's efforts are successful, others may decide to follow; those firms with something to hide will find it lonely in the shadows.

Source: The Economist, *16 May 1998, p. 97*

Although there is still some way to go on financial accounting switching to economic income in Annual Reports, the concept of economic income is now commonly used in the financial markets when analysing firms' performance. Economic income is the same thing as **economic value added**, which, as we mentioned in the Introduction, was popularised by consultants Stern Stewart with the trademark **EVA**. Stern Stewart advocate that entities should concentrate on maximising EVA where EVA = E in our equations.

Equation (5) can be written:

$$V_t = A_t + \sum_{n=1}^{\infty} \frac{\text{EVA}_{t+n}}{(1 + \text{WACC})^n} \tag{6}$$

Where

$$\text{EVA}_t = \text{NOPAT}_t - \text{WACC} \times A_{t-1} \tag{7a}$$

$$= (\text{ROCE}_t - \text{WACC}) \times A_{t-1} \tag{7b}$$

and

ROCE_t = Return on capital employed in period t measured by NOPAT_t/A_{t-1}

They argue, from equation (6), that it is clear that maximising future EVAs will have a direct impact on value, V_t. Equations (6) and (7) also spell out a financial strategy for the firm:

- Concentrate on those activities which produce positive EVAs, that is, which earn ROCE in excess of the WACC.

- Dispose of those activities which produce negative EVAs, that is, which earn ROCE less than the WACC.

- Minimise WACC.

The attractions of the EVA formula are twofold. First, as can be seen above, it is simple to understand and relatively straightforward to translate into financial objectives. Senior executives such as those at Disney and Merck in the USA and Boots and Lucas Varity in the UK have been in the vanguard of firms adopting this change in financial objectives, away from earnings per share and towards maximising EVA through maximising ROCE and minimising WACC.

Second, it is a market value-related measure which can be expressed entirely in terms of accounting numbers available both in financial accounts and management accounts and is a measure which can be used both by investors external to the organisation and by senior executives and internal divisional managers.

Exercise 3.1

Given that managers are being judged by EVA, what would be the impact on the EVA numbers if interest rates and hence the WACC were to fall, as happened in the late 1990s? Should managers be rewarded or penalised for this?

Economic income in internal reporting

Economic income-based measures are also gaining popularity for use in internal reporting and performance measurement as can be seen from a survey of UK firms carried out by Spencer and Francis (1998). The results of their survey are shown in Table 3.1.

Although profit-based measures still dominate divisional performance measurement in the UK, the new value-based measures such as EVA and shareholder value analysis (SVA) are being considered by a number of organisations.

However, UK corporates have been less eager to embrace these new measures than their US counterparts. This is partly due to a lack of awareness, as demonstrated by Table 3.1, and partly due to a reticence to implement measures which have not yet stood the test of time.

Table 3.1   The use of divisional financial performance measures in the UK

Survey of 296 UK members of the Chartered Institute of Management Accountants (CIMA)

	Used %	Being considered %	Not being considered %	Not aware of %
Ability to stay within budget	99	1	0	0
Balanced Scorecard approach	24	21	29	26
Economic Value Added (EVA®)	10	18	46	26
Residual Income (RI)	6	2	56	36
Return on Capital Employed	71	6	18	5
Shareholder Value Analysis (SVA)	15	13	53	19
Target cash flow	70	7	17	6
Target profit	94	3	2	1
Value drivers	28	18	35	19

Source: Spencer and Francis, 1998

In the USA, value-based performance measures are increasingly being adopted by managers for internal use (Ryan and Trahan, 1997).

These are:

- net present value (NPV)
- return on invested capital (ROIC) or cash flow return on investment (CFROI)
- economic value added (EVA).

The value-based performance measures, explained below, all relate to economic income by including some allowance for the capital used in generating returns.

The first value-based performance measure, NPV, has been the preferred decision rule for capital budgeting decisions where project cash flows are estimated for the life of the project – which can be many years – and then discounted by a discount rate based on the WACC to give a net present value. In theory, the NPV of a project is the amount which will be added to the entity value as soon as the project is undertaken and is an

For discussion of the balanced scorecard approach see the article by Kaplan and Norton in the Course Reader.

economic value in the sense that it allows for the cost of any capital required. The NPV measure satisfies many of the criteria described in the Dillon and Owers' quote in Section 3.2 on the requirement for management accounting metrics. However, it has one major flaw. It is a pure cash-flow measure which does not fit neatly into the accounting data provided by the traditional management accounting system and this explains, for example, why *ex post* audit of projects is rarely carried out in a systematic manner as it is difficult to compare forecast cash-flow data with actual accounting data.

The other value-based performance measures have the advantage of being able to slot into management accounting systems as they use accounting data already available within the internal reporting system. In fact, all are accounting approximations of measures of economic returns. None of them in practice is as closely correlated with value as is discounted cash flow since each uses accounting estimates of cash flow.

However, they are a compromise between a true value performance measure such as NPV and a pure accounting measure such as earnings and are designed to work not just at the external director/shareholder level but also at the director/divisional manager level. And they are increasingly used to motivate divisional manager performance in line with companies' strategic objectives.

Table 3.2 gives brief definitions of the four performance measures discussed in this section.

Table 3.2	Performance measures definitions
NPV	The free cash flows less the cost of the investment discounted to a net present value at the organisation's or division's cost of capital less the cost of the investment
ROIC	The return from net operating profit less adjusted taxes as a percentage of opening or average invested capital
CFROI	The discount rates at which the net present value of the inflation-adjusted cash flows available to capital holders equals the value of the invested capital. It is effectively the real IRR of the investment
EVA	The excess of the operating profit net of adjusted taxes created during the year over the money cost of invested capital

ROIC is the Return on Invested Capital where return is calculated as the net operating profit after adjusted taxes (NOPAT, as if there were no debt) and invested capital is the opening or average capital over the year provided by long-term investors. These long-term investors are deemed to include long-term debt and equity providers but may also include providers of short-term debt finance if this is a consistent source of financing. ROIC is a version of return on capital employed, is at the entity level, and has an adjustment to the tax number to separate the return calculation from the financing decision by adjusting the tax payment to be the tax which would be paid if there were no debt in the capital structure.

CFROI is the Cash Flow Return on Investment and is forecast into the future as well as calculated for the present and the past. CFROI is also a rate of return along the lines of return on capital employed, but here cash flow (earnings plus interest paid plus depreciation and other basic adjustments for non-cash flow items less adjusted taxes) is used in preference to accounting profit in the numerator. The numbers are inflation-adjusted to allow year-on-year comparisons of underlying performance unaffected by the rate of inflation. Since CFROI is expressed in real terms, it has to be compared with the cost of capital also in real terms. CFROI also separates the cash flows from a business into two elements: those generated from existing assets and those expected to be generated from future asset investments. The cash flows from future investments are assumed to go through a competitive life cycle with the CFROI eventually falling to the real cost of capital. Existing assets are also forecast to wind down over the economic life of those assets. In this way, CFROI can be forecast into the future and can be used not only as a historic performance measure but as a means of valuing companies. EVA is a money amount rather than a ratio and allows for the cost of capital by subtracting from NOPAT a charge for capital estimated at WACC times the invested capital. The three measures are in essence based on the same two accounting figures, NOPAT and invested capital. They are merely versions of the same approach marketed by different consultants.

For example, suppose that a firm in one year has NOPAT of £10 million, invested capital of £80 million and a WACC of 10%. CFROI and ROIC would be 10/80 or 12.5%, which is higher than the WACC of 10%. EVA would be £10m – (10% × £80m) = £2m. The company could be said to have added £2m of economic value in that year – which should be directly reflected in the market value of the entity. If, however, NOPAT had been £5m that year, £3m of economic value would have been destroyed. In order to increase future EVA, managers would have to increase NOPAT by improving asset turnover or return on assets to improve ROCE; reduce WACC, say by increasing their debt; or reduce the amount of invested capital by selling unprofitable divisions.

> This is a very simple example, ignoring the subtle difference between CFROI and ROIC.

However, despite the simplicity of EVA as a concept and the fact that it relies only on accounting numbers, there are two main disadvantages to EVA.

The first disadvantage is that using EVA to compare companies, as investors are likely to do, on an annual basis, is likely to lead to invidious comparisons. NOPAT is an accounting approximation of cash flow and so may mislead unless a number of years' EVAs are considered. Consider for example, the criticism of EVA put forward in Box 3.4 by Roger Carr, CEO of Williams Holdings, a firm which suffers from being measured on EVA on an annual and historic basis rather than the present value of expected EVAs as the valuation formula (6) suggests.

BOX 3.4   TOWARDS A TRUER MEASURE OF VALUE

You know the search for the holy grail in valuation has reached new proportions when stockbrokers devote increasing resources to identifying new methods by which to measure shareholder value.

How should we measure the value created by companies – by profits, earnings per share, cash flow or return on capital?

During the history of my company, Williams, the international manufacturing group, investment analysis has seen the rise and fall in popularity of several methods.

The traditional measures of earnings per share, dividend per share and dividend yield appear to remain popular, and Williams has fared well on these analyses: since 1993 it has delivered total earnings per share growth of 15 per cent and total dividend per share growth of 14 per cent, resulting in a dividend yield of 5.7 per cent in 1995.

However, operating performance ratios based on cash flow and capital efficiency have risen in status. Williams has been a strong cash generator, with operating cash flow over the past two years averaging 116 per cent of operating profit.

This has been achieved while the group has maintained among the highest dividend payouts in the sector and capital expenditure a full 10 per cent ahead of depreciation. The group has also achieved an unusually high return on operating assets of nearly 40 per cent. Return on sales and working capital ratios, which form a picture of profitability and cash flow, have also proved to be further popular performance ratios for investors.

Return on sales analysis of businesses acquired by Williams reveals that average margins rose from 8 per cent to 15 per cent under Williams.

Working capital ratios highlight ability to keep a tight control on working capital – the average working capital turn averaged four times a year for companies acquired by the group. But this rose to more than 7.5 times in 1995, mainly due to an early commitment to short-cycle manufacturing.

The most recent valuation method of operating performance to increase in popularity among analysts, companies and financial journalists has been economic value added (EVA), which measures the return on capital and its cost.

An article in the *Financial Times* on October 7 reported that under EVA analysis Williams was seen to have a disappointing record on shareholder value. It highlighted the value of EVA in altering the philosophy of both managers' and investors' thinking to recognise that the capital employed in a business is not free.

In other words, a company's cost of capital and the difference between that and its return must play an important role in any analysis of whether a company is creating value. On first analysis, all very plausible. However, just as in the case of other valuation measures, so EVA also has its pitfalls.

First, it has been rightly pointed out by Paul Marsh, professor at the London Business School, that the crucial calculation of the cost of capital 'is not a precise science', but secondly and more importantly, it must be recognised that EVA is a snapshot of a company's capital efficiency taken over a one-year timeframe. This is potentially distorting as it takes no account of such factors as significant investments, acquisitions or disposals during the year or indeed the speed at which prior acquisitions contribute to earnings.

The second weakness lies in the issue of goodwill.

Goodwill is indeed the natural consequence of acquiring and developing high-quality businesses. The added value created by a company while a business is under its management control only becomes fully evident in the goodwill premium achieved when a business is sold.

This is illustrated by the announcement made by Williams last week that it has agreed to sell 15 of its building product companies for £360m – at a premium of more than £90m to what was originally paid. This premium was reflected in an internal rate of return for the businesses of at least 13 per cent net of tax during the time they were under Williams's management. When taking risk and reward into account, this would be considered a reasonable return on any investor's criteria.

At December 31 1995, the majority of these companies had been under Williams management for seven to eight years during which time the annual profitability rose by 88 per cent, return on sales rose 68 per cent to an average of 12 per cent and the return on capital employed improved by 60 per cent to an annual rate of 32 per cent.

On the basis of these figures it is clear that Williams created added performance value on behalf of shareholders during that time. The full increase in shareholder value, however, only came to light in EVA terms when those companies were sold and the value of management effort in developing the businesses was revealed in the increase in goodwill value. The evidence, then, may point to the fact that the search for a holy grail of performance analysis may indeed be a vain one. As each valuation method presents its own advantages and limitations, it is perhaps worth emphasising that the bedrock on which shareholder assessment of any business should be built remains the clarity of corporate strategy and quality of management.

Source: Financial Times, *11 November 1996*

Activity 3.3

Do you think that Carr's criticisms of EVA in Box 3.4 are valid?

Senior managers are masters of the art of presenting company performance in the desired light and we must always apply our best critical examination to arguments that may be self-serving. The two problems mentioned are not the conceptual flaws Carr implies but merely difficulties in carrying out EVA. On the first point, EVA does in fact take into account investments made during the year. Of course, if they are added to the balance sheet at historic value, then the future benefit will not be reflected. But if the future earning power from the investment is very likely to create value then it could be incorporated in the valuation. If not, it would make more sense to wait until the asset has generated value before recognising it. In either case, EVA works. The same response applies to the point about goodwill. If the subsidiaries disposed of did actually gain value during the period, then it is the aim of EVA to establish the gain and recognise it. If the disposal price was high merely because the purchaser identified synergy and

paid more than the business was worth to Williams, then it would be
appropriate to say the value was only created at the time of the disposal, and
that is when EVA will recognise it.

In addition, invested capital is determined from companies' balance
sheets and different accounting policies will lead to different values for
invested capital. We saw in Unit 6 how using book value as a method of
company valuation might under- or over-estimate current values of
capital employed in a business and these potential discrepancies apply
equally to estimates of invested capital for EVA purposes. Stern Stewart
acknowledge that up to 164 accounting adjustments should be made to
book values in order to estimate current values of invested capital (Stern
et al., 1995) but the three main adjustments to be made to rectify
breaches of the clean surplus income rule are:

- Accumulated goodwill written off should be added to invested capital
  and, if deducted from profits, added back to NOPAT. This adjustment
  recognises that companies which have been acquired should be
  included at the full price paid rather than at the book value at the
  time of the acquisition. They should earn a return above WACC on
  their true rather than their book cost.

- Research and development expenditure should be treated as an asset
  rather than an expense. In the same way as goodwill, it should be
  added back to NOPAT and included as part of invested capital, albeit
  depreciated more rapidly than goodwill.

- Leases should be treated as part of debt finance and hence as part of
  invested capital. Operating lease payments should be added back to
  NOPAT and the off-balance sheet value of operating leases added to
  invested capital. Finance leases are already capitalised under most
  accounting policies.

BOX 3.5   WHAT'S IT ALL ABOUT, EVA?

EVA may look interesting in theory. But how easy
is it to apply? Here we show how to calculate Glaxo
Wellcome's EVA for the year to December 1995.

To begin with, we have to get a better idea of
Glaxo's economic value by bringing its balance
sheet up to date. The two largest adjustments are
goodwill and R&D. Following its acquisition of
Wellcome, Glaxo wrote off over £5bn of goodwill.
Since that reflects what Wellcome is really worth,
we added it back to Glaxo's shareholders' funds.

Glaxo also spends over £1bn a year on R&D, which
it writes off against profits. Since this is aimed at
developing new drugs, EVA suggests it should be
treated as an asset. So we worked out Glaxo's R&D
spending for the past four years, and added it back.

Finally, since a company's employed capital is
put to work regardless of how it is funded, we also
added Glaxo's total debt and its minority interests
to its capital.

Now we can work out what Glaxo's assets earned
in 1995. This is defined as its operating profit after tax.
However, profit figures can be distorted by charges.
In 1995, Glaxo set aside over £1.2bn to fund
Wellcome's integration. But the lion's share was
merely added to provisions, and was not spent in
1995. So we added the movement in provisions back
to profits. Similarly, we have already capitalised past
R&D costs as an asset on the balance sheet. So
Glaxo's 1995 outlay has to be added back as well.

Now we can calculate Glaxo Wellcome's return
on capital. In 1995, we find it earned a healthy 29.5
per cent return.

But working out the return on capital is only the
first step. We now have to find out how much
Glaxo's capital costs. That means looking at the
cost of debt and equity.

The cost of debt is simply the average interest
rate the company pays. Glaxo Wellcome pays an
average interest rate of just 7 per cent.

EVA uses the capital asset pricing model to work
out the cost of equity. [...] Applying the model to
Glaxo produces a cost of equity of 13.8 per cent.
That's cheap because historically Glaxo's shares
have been pacific relative to the market.

Finally, we have to weight the costs of equity and
debt relative to their use by Glaxo. About 70 per
cent of its capital is equity and the rest debt, so the
weighting produces a cost of 11.5 per cent.

From these figures, we can see that Glaxo's
return on capital exceeded its cost of capital by 18
per cent in 1995. That year, it certainly succeeded
in creating value for its shareholders.

Source: Investors Chronicle, *17 January 1997*

Exercise 3.2 _____

Consider a retail chain such as Boots. Boots chooses to lease a large number of its shops and, since property leases are operating leases, this means that these assets and associated financing are off-balance sheet. We saw in Unit 6, Section 2.2, how Boots' capital employed, or invested capital, could be adjusted by capitalising the operating leases. What would this do to Boots ROCE and EVA calculations?

The second main disadvantage of EVA is that, in practice, it is difficult to implement at the divisional level. Traditional divisional performance measures concentrated on profit measures and so divisional estimates of NOPAT are in most organisations already available. Also, we have seen how to adjust WACC for divisional risk in Unit 4, Section 4.4, and this can be done relatively simply by the finance department using betas from comparable organisations and adjusting where appropriate for different divisional capital structures. The main difficulty in applying EVA at the divisional level is in how to apportion invested capital at appropriate values across divisions and this can take many months of consultant time.

Guinness, now a subsidiary of Diageo, complained how difficult it would be to apportion the value of whisky stocks in bond in Scotland between 96 different country managers!

The use of divisional performance measures, whatever they may be, has the inherent disadvantage of potentially misallocating resource and EVA is no exception. Transfer pricing choices between divisions will affect NOPAT and hence EVA and there are circumstances when, for tax or legal reasons, or because the true transfer price is difficult to determine, divisional EVA estimates will be misleading in terms of strategic decision-making (Zimmerman, 1997). However, this divisional allocation has to be done in order to force middle managers to be aware of the value of capital employed in generating profits and to be able to estimate whether economic income or EVA is positive or negative. Under a simple profit target system, unproductive assets might still add to profits. Under an EVA approach, unproductive assets which do not earn their required return reduce EVA and should therefore be sold.

One final criticism of EVA, and of value-based metrics in general, is that they have as yet failed to take account of the changes in the nature of capital employed in many firms. Intellectual capital, in the form of training expenditure and spending on IT systems and knowledge data banks, is not yet included in balance sheets nor in adjusted estimates of invested capital. It is only included if firms with intellectual capital have been acquired, when it appears as goodwill. There is at the time of writing a feeling that new performance measures may be required in future years which take account not just of shareholder value and physical assets but also of a wider range of stakeholders and assets such as employees (who are not yet treated as 'tangibles' or 'intangibles' for accounting purposes!).

'This view of the corporation as accountable to a broad range of social interests also leads to a different way of evaluating corporate performance. In the past it has been customary to focus on the profits earned by a particular company. But there is another measure of corporate success that may be more relevant: namely the total social benefits derived from a corporation's activity net of any social disadvantages. For example, in developing *internal* measures of performance, corporations may choose increasingly to capitalize rather than expense their outlays on training, software and R&D. Such outlays represent investments in the corporate future, and corporate *internal* accounting (and perhaps external accounting, too) should recognise these realities of the new management era.'

Jochi Aoi, Chairman of the Board, Toshiba Corporation, in 'To Whom does the Company Belong?: A New Management Mission for the Information Age.' pp. 247–8.

Source: Chew, 1997

Until performance measures which are relevant to a wider range of stakeholders have been devised, research is being concentrated on studying how good value-based measures such as EVA are, not just within the company to see if managers are being encouraged to maximise shareholder wealth when being judged by such performance measures, but also at the share price level to see if they are predictors of future share price performance. There is conflicting evidence so far, partly hindered by the fact that consultants are carrying out research for which they have a vested interest in obtaining 'helpful' results and also because there is disagreement on methodology.

There is no doubt, however, that value-based measures are here to stay and have had a major impact on corporate strategy, management remuneration and financial policy. Not least, they have tried and to some extent succeeded in bridging the traditional gap between management accounts, financial accounts, and corporate finance.

Activity 3.4

Read the *Economist* article entitled 'A star to sail by' on EVA and other performance measures in the Course Reader.

Before we leave the subject of internal and external accounting, and by way of an introduction to Section 4, 'Public-sector financial management', one of the interesting global developments in this area is the spread of performance measures to the public sector. In the next section, we will look in more detail at the role of public-sector accounting in terms of control and performance measures but we briefly outline the main changes here.

Pressure has been mounting in most countries for governments to curb public spending. Alternatives such as raising taxes or increasing public-sector debt are limited and many governments have turned to cost savings, particularly in administration, as a more palatable solution. Historically, government spending has been monitored and reported on a **cash accounting** basis, with capital spending rationed through control of capital expenditure budgets. Cash accounts do not differentiate between spending on one-off items and spending on assets which can generate future revenues. Cash accounting can therefore lead to under-investment if capital is rationed. On the other hand, once assets have been acquired, there is no incentive under cash accounting to dispose of loss-making ones, since there is no apparent cost to keeping them.

In an attempt to control spending and improve the efficiency of resource allocation, governments have begun to turn to **accruals accounting**. Under such a system, government departments and other public-sector organisations, such as NHS trusts, account for capital investments in the conventional private-sector way, that is, they acquire them as assets and

Accruals accounting is a method of accounting which tries to match income and related expenses in the same accounting period. You should be familiar with this concept from your studies of previous courses. In the UK local authorities have a modified form of accrual accounting and the NHS adopted accrual accounting in 1991.

then, in future years, apply a capital charge to income to take account of the resources used. This is equivalent to the concept of economic income described above, the differences being that, in the public sector, the WACC is replaced by a government-determined cost of capital and estimates of invested capital may be less complex than in the private sector.

This approach was adopted in the early to mid-nineties with some success, as in this example from New Zealand:

> Information on assets and liabilities, which accrual accounting provides, is needed to monitor aspects of the ownership interest such as financial viability, return on investment, and maintenance of capital.
>
> Accrual accounting, in conjunction with the system of capital charges, means that departments must record assets and that their ongoing costs include both depreciation and the opportunity cost of capital.
>
> With balance sheets in place, the new regime has been able to introduce incentives for better asset management.
>
> *(Pallot and Ball, 1997)*

At the time of writing, accruals accounting is being introduced in the UK public sector through what is known as **resource accounting**. This uses accruals-based accounting techniques to produce five different statements for central government departments and executive agencies. The statements are:

* operating statement
* balance sheet
* cash-flow statement
* a main objective analysis
* output and performance analysis.

Under resource accounting, UK central government departments and executive agencies must set out their performance indicators. There is currently dispute as to which parts of the above statements will be audited (although the financial parts will certainly be audited). The benefits claimed for resource accounting are:

* introduction of generally accepted accounting practice (GAAP)
* better management information
* inputs matched to outputs
* improved information on assets
* improved resource allocation.

These advantages were set out in a UK Government white paper called 'Better Accounting for the Taxpayer's Money' (HM Treasury, 1995). Budgeting on an accrual basis is due to follow.

Notice how governments as well as the private sector are switching from control of cash inputs to monitoring of outputs. However, governments have made less progress than the private sector in linking performance relative to these benchmarks to executive pay. This has been done in the privatised companies but to a much lesser extent in organisations still fully owned or controlled by the state. Section 4 will elaborate on the changing nature of public financial control and the increased emphasis on performance measurement of outcomes in the public sector. It will also use as a case study the privatisation of part of the UK rail network.

This case study highlights who may benefit when performance exceeds expectations.

SUMMARY

In this section, we have looked at internal reporting and external reporting, otherwise known as management accounting and financial accounting respectively, in terms of their functions. Management accounting has three main functions: planning, decision-making and control; financial accounting also has three main functions: decision-making, stewardship and accountability.

We then looked at how the control function of both internal and external reporting have been replaced by a concentration on performance measures and how the performance measures used to judge senior managers are increasingly being applied within the divisions of an organisation and being tied to remuneration schemes.

Another trend has been a shift away from emphasis on accounting income towards measuring economic income, that is, income after allowing for an appropriate charge on capital. This has been popularised under the name EVA but a number of other value-based performance measures are also in use, all of which use accounting surrogates of cash flow and take into account the cost of capital in an attempt to improve the efficiency of resource use. These measures are also now being applied in the public sector, notably in New Zealand, (see Pallot and Ball, 1997) and, increasingly, in the UK.

4 AUDIT AND ACCOUNTABILITY IN THE PUBLIC SECTOR

4.1   Definitions of value-for-money auditing   **42**

4.2   The future of value-for-money auditing   **54**

4.3   Best value   **55**

        Summary   **56**

In this section, we turn our attention to governance and financial management in the public sector. In particular we examine how more effective financial management and accountability can be driven by **value for money** (**VFM**). Whilst the examples given here relate to the public sector there are many lessons that can be applied to any sector. This section also includes a case study that uses extracts from a UK National Audit Office (NAO) report on whether the true value was obtained from a sale of government assets. However, VFM is not simply a UK phenomenon, as will be illustrated by the international examples given.

You should be familiar with the term value for money from your previous studies. Value-for-money auditing is the process by which the three E's (Economy, Efficiency and Effectiveness) are examined.

In recent years governments have striven to achieve greater financial control of their activities in order to control government spending and to improve resource allocation and accountability. This has resulted in a number of innovations, such as: privatisation; the Private Finance Initiative; the move from cash to accruals accounting; resource accounting; and changes to the way the public sector is audited.

Public-sector auditing has a wider purpose than does private-sector external auditing, where audit tends to focus on stewardship and accountability in terms of financial reporting. Public-sector audit seeks to improve resource allocation and organisational performance as well as performing an accountability and stewardship function.

BOX 4.1   THE ROLE OF THE NATIONAL AUDIT OFFICE AND THE AUDIT COMMISSION

In England and Wales the statutory authority to conduct VFM studies was granted in 1982 for local government and 1983 for central government. The main public-sector external auditors in Britain are the National Audit Office, the Audit Commission for England and Wales and the Accounts Commission for Scotland. The National Audit Office audits central government and The Audit Commission is responsible for local government and the National Health Service. VFM audits are undertaken by the internal audit function (which is statutory for most UK public sector organisations) and also by management as part of their performance review function.

It has been claimed that a form of 'value for money' auditing has been with us since the fifth century BC (Dewar, 1989). However its application has only become widespread during the last two decades. Normanton (1966) argued that VFM auditing was a response to 'big government' in the twentieth century; and that it 'make[s] a growing contribution to the development of public administration and government as a whole – a contribution which no other organ of the state could possibly make'. But just when VFM auditing has firmly established itself in the public sector, the world it inhabits has changed and the need for and the role of VFM auditing is in dispute. Power (1994) suggests two extremes of the need for audit in general: on the one hand it can be argued that audit is a central part of the 'reinvention of government'; on the other hand VFM audit can appear intrusive and out of step with a culture where managers are encouraged to be responsible for their own performance.

Part of the confusion lies in the fact that the objectives, methodology and audit standards for VFM auditing vary between and within the audit bodies, and differ further between client groups and national contexts. Looking back over the last few decades, it is possible to identify different approaches to VFM auditing and to some extent to match these to certain sets of circumstances. This review suggests an evolution of VFM audit from a 'hands on' approach where auditors confronted managers and the public with examples of waste and inefficiency, to a more refined form whereby the VFM ethos has empowered managers and the auditors are consigned to their familiar role of checking management's account of VFM achievements.

BOX 4.2   THE ORIGINS OF VFM AUDITING

In England, it is doubtful whether the idea of an audit going beyond consideration of regularity (i.e., checking for the presence of any irregularities) was ever even considered in the early days of parliamentary control of accounts. An interesting insight into some of the early VFM auditing in the UK, from an 1887 audit report, involved the purchase of ribbon for army medals for 20 shillings when it could have been purchased from another supplier for 14 shillings. This case pushed the boundary of auditing beyond regularity. The military department initially refused to reply to the report thus provoking a landmark declaration from the Committee of Public Accounts: 'If in the course of his audit, the auditor becomes aware of facts which appear to him to indicate an improper expenditure or waste of public money it is his duty to call the attention of Parliament to this.' (Normanton, 1966).

Despite occasional investigations of this type, audit remained mainly of the regularity variety until the late 1940s when the growth in expenditure following the Second World War was matched by a similar extension of the volume and range of VFM reports. Pallot (1991) associates the increased emphasis on VFM auditing with increasing concerns about government expenditure in the 1960s and 1970s which caused government auditors to take a wider perspective and to re-orientate the audit approach towards 'comprehensive' or 'integrated' audits.

Good quality medal ribbons were clearly a vital military accessory

4.1 DEFINITIONS OF VALUE-FOR-MONEY AUDITING

There is no general agreement of what the term 'value for money audit' actually means. INTOSAI's (United Nations) notion of an 'expanded scope' audit introduces the concept of auditing management activities 'There is another type of audit which is oriented towards performance, effectiveness, economy and efficiency of public administration. This audit includes not only specific aspects of management, but comprehensive management activities, including organisation and administrative systems' (INTOSAI, 1977).

In the USA, the General Accounting Office (1988) audit standards take this a step further and discuss performance auditing as including 'the extent to which desired results or benefits ... are being achieved ... whether the objectives of a proposed, new or ongoing program are proper, suitable or relevant'.

It is generally acknowledged that, as a minimum, VFM audit includes an examination of economy, efficiency and effectiveness. Sharkansky (1991) discusses the different labels given to the activity (e.g. the three E's, value for money, operational auditing, effectiveness auditing, performance auditing, programme results auditing) and comments that 'While some may emphasise the nuances that distinguish these labels and what they signify, their communality lies in their concern with judging the quality of governmental activities as opposed to the auditor's classic concern with financial records.' The term 'value for money' will, therefore, be used here as a convenient expression and embracing VFM in its widest possible sense – to embrace everything from economy to policy.

Activity 4.1

You may find it useful to look back at your previous studies of the three E's either in Book 4 of B800 or in Block 6 of B752, depending on the route you have taken.

The Three E's defined

Economy: *Obtaining appropriate resources at minimum cost*

Efficiency: *Obtaining maximum output from a given level of resources*

            Or

            Requiring minimum input of resources for a given level of output

Effectiveness: *Achieving organisational objectives*

When the definition of VFM audit is so broad-based and difficult to pin down it is unsurprising that different audit bodies in different countries use a variety of approaches to implement VFM audit. In discussing VFM audit it may be helpful to distinguish between these different approaches. It is possible to identify six different types (see Table 4.1). This list is not intended to be exhaustive nor does it imply that the auditor must select just one approach. Different types of audit may be selected for different projects and an individual audit may even feature aspects of several approaches. With the possible exception of 'comparative audit', the different approaches can be seen as representing the evolutionary development of VFM auditing, from review of management systems through to the quality audit. It would seem that the involvement of the auditor has an interactive effect with management systems and that, as these systems have improved, the auditor has been able to move on to the next, possibly more efficient, audit approach.

Table 4.1   Six approaches to value for money auditing
1   Review of management systems, arrangements and procedures
Auditor identifies poor value for money, makes recommendations for improvement and gives advice on management arrangements to improve value for money
2   The value for money procedures audit
Auditor checks that an organisation has established objectives, has systems for measuring performance and for ensuring that objectives have been achieved
3   Policy audit
Auditor assesses whether a policy or programme has been effective as well as economical and efficient
4   Audit of management representations of value for money
Auditor verifies information prepared by management on the achievement of value for money
5   Comparative performance audit
Auditor compiles a database to compare cost/performance between similar organisations, identifies and recommends best practice to improve value for money
6   Quality audit
Auditor uses customer satisfaction surveys to evaluate successful performance; may also verify management's quality assurance information

Source: Bowerman (1996)

Although these approaches represent developments through time it does not mean that the earlier approaches are no longer used. The main determining features which influence the approach selected for a particular project include:

- To what extent may the auditor question policy?
- To what extent is an issue policy-sensitive?
- How much management information is available?

We shall now consider in detail each of these six approaches.

1   Review of management systems, arrangements and procedures

There are two possible stages to this approach, the first being to identify examples of bad VFM and the second being to examine if management arrangements are adequate to secure good VFM.

(a) An individual study, which brings to light examples of waste and inefficiency, usually within a fairly narrow area of management activity such as: property, control of capital projects, purchasing, stores and energy conservation or particular services within a department. These are intended to lead to savings or improvements in areas studied. This was the style of most 'early' VFM audits and remains a good standby for impact and media attention. For example it was suggested that the UK Ministry of Defence could save £7m on unused or redundant telephone lines. The NAO defines this type of audit as 'selective investigations of signs of possible serious waste, extravagance, inefficiency, ineffectiveness or weaknesses in control'.

(b) The review approach is sometimes extended to include an examination of the arrangements or systems that would normally be expected to be present in order to secure VFM. During the 1980s, audit organisations began to undertake audits of management arrangements to provide assurance and without necessarily uncovering a particular problem. This approach shares features of a (financial) internal controls review. The auditors may review planning and budgeting systems, decision-making processes, stores procurement, maintenance of buildings and regulations for planning, tendering, etc. This type of audit is typified by what the NAO describes as 'good housekeeping', which means: 'Major reviews of standard managerial operations that tend to follow common patterns or procedures or established good practice.' This approach is also used in Canada. For example, the Canadian Auditor General (1992) found that the Department of National Health and Welfare's policy and procedures 'do not ensure that disability benefits are paid only to those who continue to be eligible due to severe and prolonged disability'.

It is arguable that this type of audit has largely fulfilled its purpose. Over the years, the advice given and the embarrassment caused by adverse audit reports have served to encourage management to put their own houses in order. As managers assume responsibility for their organisation's performance, this type of audit is likely to be seen as intrusive and as second-guessing management. The auditors themselves may appear guilty of ineffectiveness. The NAO's reports on the Gulf War drew criticisms of lack of understanding of the difficulties facing the British Army in a war situation.

This approach has also been accused of causing managers to view VFM audit as an adversarial process rather than something that requires mutual respect and co-operation. The reluctance of the auditors to let go of this area may be because they view the 'holding to account' as an important aspect of VFM audit. If they do not uncover waste which later comes to light, they could be accused of not doing their jobs properly. In addition, such studies do hit the headlines and are a way in which audit bodies can demonstrate their 'success'.

2   The value for money procedures audit

Again there are potentially two stages to this approach. The first concentrates on the way the department measures its own VFM, the second extends the audit examination to arrive at a judgement on whether or not VFM has been achieved.

(a) This approach to VFM auditing may be seen as a response to the absence of reliable and meaningful performance data on public bodies. This is at the heart of the NAO's approach to its 'major broad based investigations of a whole audited body, activity, project or programme investigating implementation and results'. The procedures audit is 'to examine how well ... systems and controls operate, and whether they provide management with the necessary information to monitor performance satisfactorily [and to] assess, against predetermined criteria, whether VFM is being achieved ... [and to] make recommendations for improvements and to work with the body to improve financial control and VFM'. Many NAO reports are of this style, for example questioning the effectiveness of cervical and breast cancer screening by reference to established objectives and systems for measuring performance. A review of sickness absence at the Inland Revenue found that although appropriate management arrangements were in place it was difficult to judge their impact on productivity and sickness absence levels as there was no mechanism to monitor the outcome of these activities. The Canadian Auditor General (1992) also takes this approach, for example to address the question: 'Is the government making progress in environmental protection?'. He concludes: 'The government and its partners will have to continue to work at developing indicators against which progress can be measured ... there are gaps in environmental data ... it is sometimes difficult to define acceptable standards of environmental quality. There must be complete, clear, concise, honest and accurate reporting of results against proposed targets, if Canadians are to be able to judge the success or failure of efforts to protect the environment'.

The emphasis of such studies is to check that management has established procedures, to provide assurance, not necessarily to highlight waste.

(b) An extension of the role is to evaluate whether or not VFM has been achieved. This is dependent partly on whether objectives have been defined and whether the data are available. In some cases, studies do reveal that waste or loss has occurred; e.g. under-pricing of the electricity companies may have resulted in the tax payer losing out on as much as £600m (NAO, 1992).

The topic of privatisation under-pricing is also dealt with later in Box 4.3.

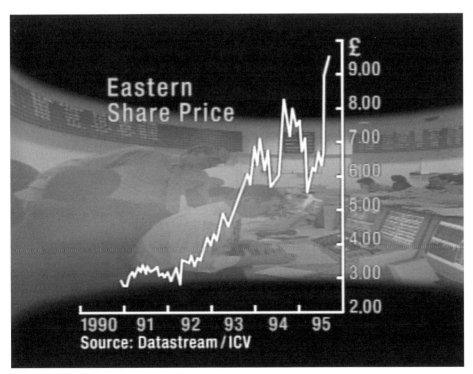

Post-privatisation value-added for shareholders. What about tax-payers?

However, if adequate management arrangements and procedures for measuring VFM are in place then the report usually implies that there is no blame to be apportioned, only lessons to be learnt.

The willingness of the auditor to judge achievement of VFM also depends on the political sensitivity of the potential conclusions. In general the auditors tend to stop short of giving an opinion on the overall ineffectiveness of a programme in these types of study.

This approach can run into difficulty if politicians do not set clear policy objectives and in the real world there may not always be a neat, rational and systematic statement of objectives for every area. If the auditors press for such a statement to be provided they may be accused of interfering in policy and they may be tempted to confine their investigation to clear-cut cases where the facts speak for themselves rather than seeking to establish a link between ministerial policy objectives and results. Furthermore, in the contract culture it may appear outmoded to place emphasis on procedures, systems and central guidance rather than on the results achieved. Under new-style public management, responsibility for results lies down the line with management not up the line with politicians.

3   Policy audit

A policy audit questions whether a policy or programme has been effective as well as economical and efficient. The extent to which the auditor can question policy is the most fraught issue in VFM auditing. In most countries policy is the responsibility of elected representatives and the legislature and, while the auditors can examine how policy has been implemented, they may not question the merits of policy. Radford (1991) contends that this is 'a distinction without a difference, for to comment on the outcome of a particular policy can be tantamount to passing an opinion on the merits of the policy itself'. Therefore, there is as yet no distinguishable approach to the audit of policy. However, there is increasing evidence that auditors are involved in the questioning and even in the creation of policy.

The Canadian Auditor General has occasionally been quite closely involved in policy issues; in his 1992 report he reprimands the government for a three-year delay in implementing staffing policies: 'legislative change is needed and is long overdue – the status quo is unacceptable'. In the UK, the Audit Commission has on occasion criticised central government for their lack of progress on community care. Describing government support for urban regeneration as 'a patchwork quilt of complexity and idiosyncrasy', it expressed the view that there were 'serious drawbacks to the [community] charge in terms of economy, efficiency and effectiveness'. Radford (1991) contends that the Audit Commission has used its position to influence the way in which local government develops. In the case of Westminster City Council, the District Auditor (appointed by the Audit Commission) went beyond merely questioning policy and actually declared the council's housing policy 'illegal': 'My provisional view is that the council was engaged in gerrymandering, which I am minded to find is a disgraceful and improper purpose' (Magill, 1994).

Gerrymander: to rearrange voting districts to favour a particular political party.

The NAO also has influenced policy through its studies. For example, its 1993 Annual Report states:

> [a] report on support for lone parent families noted that the number of lone parents receiving benefit had increased while the numbers receiving maintenance payments from liable relatives has fallen.
>
> *(National Audit Office, 1993)*

We are told that the Secretary of State subsequently announced new measures, which included the establishment of the controversial Child Support Agency. However, the NAO came much closer to policy issues in its report on the Pergau dam. The report acknowledges that it is not for the NAO to question the merits of the policy decision and so does not explicitly criticise the decision to fund the project; nevertheless the report did open up the issue of whether the project should have been funded which led to a legal challenge and a subsequent ruling that ministers had knowingly breached the terms of the 1980 Overseas Development Act.

UK Government aid for the Pergau dam project was found by the UK High Court to be illegally linked to an arms deal in a case brought by the World Development Movement in 1994.

The occasional foray into the territory of 'policy' appears to be welcomed by the public and media. This can cause disappointment when the same approach is not followed on other issues tackled by the auditors. The issue of the auditors' remit regarding policy is unlikely to be clarified through legislation but could usefully be tested more frequently by engaging in studies which confront questions of whether a particular policy has (or even will) result in VFM for the taxpayer. To ignore such questions reduces considerably the value of the audit.

4 Audit of management representations of value for money

The emphasis which new public management places on results rather than the systems by which results are achieved has created a demand in some cases for the public-sector auditor to focus on those results as presented in the audited body's Annual Report.

Policy audit under the watchful gaze of Big Ben

Canada was one of the first countries to involve the auditor in evaluating the procedures established by auditees to measure and report on the effectiveness of their programmes. The Canadian Comprehensive Auditing Foundation (1987) recommended the audit of 'management representations'; that is, of the information provided by management to their governing bodies to demonstrate their accountability.

A type of management representations audit has also been in place in New Zealand since 1989. Statements of objectives and service performance are included in the Annual Report; these measure actual outputs and compare them with outputs agreed at the start of the year. The information is intended to enable the public to learn whether organisations have provided the outputs agreed to at the beginning of the year. The New Zealand Audit Office suggests that measures should include quantity, quality, timeliness, location and cost. Initially, virtually all the authorities received qualified audits (Pallot, 1992). Typically, this was because many objectives and goals adopted were not readily measurable. However, some 'good' performance indicators were developed (e.g., to inspect 600 properties, investigate 70% of faults within a specified timescale; performance is then reported against this target giving an explanation for low success rates).

> In 1988, legislation was passed in Sweden requiring government agencies to submit output and performance data in support of their annual budget requests. Such data is subject to audit by the National Audit Bureau. Agencies are required to present results of activity broken down by operational area and to set measurable goals.
>
> *(Swedish Ministry of Finance, 1995)*

In the UK the Audit Commission has been given the responsibility to specify performance indicators for local government and to publish comparative information. Significantly, the Audit Commission must also specify information to be reported; this inevitably makes the indicators less sensitive to local circumstances and implicitly involves the auditor in deciding what constitutes 'good' performance (Bowerman, 1995). The local authority auditors are required to certify the information as genuine by examining the reliability of the systems used for collecting the data.

While audit of management representations of performance appears to be a cost-efficient approach to effectiveness auditing, there are several inherent difficulties in reporting performance in this way. First, there is the question of whether it can capture *all* aspects of performance. This is difficult to achieve because concepts of quality can be defined from different perspectives and because complex activities cannot usually be measured solely in terms of financial performance and may have to be supplemented by organisational and process-related criteria in order to obtain some indication of quality.

The second reservation concerns whether this type of audit provides useful information. For example, in the Swedish case (Swedish Ministry of Finance, 1995, p. 22) a 'clear' opinion states that: 'the National Audit Office cannot for reasons of principle apply the expression "true and fair" to the performance report. However, the disclosures provided in X's performance report do not conflict with any conditions known to the National Audit Office'.

A qualified opinion may be of more use both as an indication of and a deterrent to inadequate performance and reporting. Overall, the management representations approach is based on the premise that the information will be used by parliament and the public. However there is very little evidence that annual reports are read or used for decision-making so, ironically, the approach may make the results of VFM audit less visible. If taken to its logical conclusion it could return audit to a type of 'tick and check' function. VFM reports, which report directly on an organisation's performance, have, for all their limitations, enjoyed a much higher reputation than private-sector audit reports.

5   Comparative performance audit

The comparative performance audit involves the auditor in compiling a database to compare cost/performance between similar organisations. It can be used to assist the auditor in the selection of organisations or topics for investigation; to identify and recommend best practice to improve VFM. There is a natural link between this approach and best practice benchmarking.

A main feature of the Audit Commission's work at local and national level is its use of comparative statistical data, which provides a quantitative framework for inter-authority comparisons of performance. The Commission explains that:

> ... the distinctive feature of all this [VFM] work is that it is based on well informed comparisons between one authority and another, and on

comparisons between local performance and best practice. Locally, the aim is to adapt the lessons to the circumstances of each individual local authority. The approach is based on advice and persuasion, since auditors have no power in the VFM area to impose their views. They must work with the grain of local management.

(Audit Commission, 1991)

The approach exhibits some features of 'benchmarking' such as 'best in class' authorities and benchmarking clubs in the form of data and quality exchanges. The Audit Commission collects information on all major council and health service activities and their demographic background. This attempts to bring together all publicly available information on clients' unit costs, levels of service, staff numbers and demographic circumstances. The Commission has estimated that the task involves collecting and collating some 300,000 statistics from 30 different sources. The Commission has encouraged authorities to undertake their own performance review and has provided benchmark performance statistics supported by papers on setting up performance review mechanisms. The establishment of a quality exchange by the Audit Commission broadens the performance review to include service quality and to describe quality assurance and control techniques.

"You're going to have to lay off information."

The Audit Commission uses the comparative approach to identify best practice which forms the basis of its recommendations to all authorities; for example a report showed that £15m could be saved if hospitals mended leaking pipes and used water more efficiently. A report on education for over 16-year-olds proposed a model which could reduce the number of 'A' level failures and save up to £500m per year. Between 1983 and 1989 the Audit Commission claimed to have identified £1,328m annually recurring savings of which £662m had been achieved.

The comparative approach contrasts with the principles behind the best value approach, which we shall discuss later.

The main criticism of the comparative approach is that it gives too much emphasis to cost cutting, through its ability to single out authorities spending over the 'average'. It emphasises *economy* and *efficiency* rather than *effectiveness*. There are also problems concerning the comparability of the data; of ensuring that it reflects local circumstances and the quality of services provided. A further difficulty is that the approach can be interpreted as encroaching on policy. For example, high spending may be the result of a policy decision.

Despite these limitations, the benchmarking approach does offer benefits which could usefully be extended to other organisations whether they are in the public, private or voluntary sector. The relative prevalence of benchmarking between sectors in the UK is shown in Table 4.2.

Table 4.2   Level of benchmarking activity by sector

Sector	Percentage claiming to be benchmarking
Government	58
Education	62
Health	69
Manufacturing and construction	50
Financial services	33
Services and retailing	36
Utilities	78
Other	39
Average across sectors	47

Source: Francis et al., 1998

6   Quality audit

During the 1990s, customer satisfaction became central to management philosophy in the UK public sector. The quality approach focuses on results and on controlling the quality of output in place of bureaucratic controls that prescribe how things are done. Customer choice is encouraged through enhanced competition – 'customers reject shoddy goods and shop elsewhere' – so providers must either mend their ways or go out of business. Consumers are empowered by giving them rights to information, a complaints system and means of redress.

Concern with the customer perspective has affected audit in two ways. First, customer satisfaction levels are used to evaluate successful performance; for example, the National Audit Office in its 1993 Annual Report explains that: 'Our studies have to develop particular methods for measuring the quality of service achieved … . Frequently we have carried out our own surveys to find out what users think of the services they receive and how these might be improved.' The NAO used this approach to examine the quality of service offered by national museums and art galleries and an examination of the quality of NHS catering services.

The second potential effect would be to involve the auditor in verifying information which is provided on quality assurance. The approach is well illustrated in the Audit Commission's discussion document on its own role in health care quality assurance. The Commission proposed a variety of ways in which it could help in the quality assurance process. The proposals included the prioritising of the patient perspective and developing methods for use by NHS practitioners in assessing quality. The second set of proposals was more ambitious: it was suggested that the Commission could set themselves up as a quality assurance accreditation agency.

The use of a customer-focused approach to quality in the public sector has been criticised because it has been argued that, as services are often free and choice restricted, there is often no straightforward causal link between customer satisfaction and organisational success. Indeed, if customer satisfaction leads to increased demand, rather than adding to the success of the providing organisation by boosting business and profits, it can merely add to its troubles, because all the extra demand must be met with the same finite resources (Coote, 1994).

Furthermore, the quality approach has tended, so far, to involve consumerism and to relate to consumers in their capacity as service users. The relationships are actually more complex; for example, consumers are not the only ones who matter in schools – children, parents and employers all must be considered. As well as being interested in quality at the point of service, as citizens they are also interested in impact on the wider community in the longer term. A narrow, individualistic concept is particularly inappropriate for human welfare services. In addition, the boundary between producer and user is not absolute: for example, education requires participation by the consumer. Additionally, choice can be illusory – for example, the case of an accident and emergency service. The information provided by the auditor may be of little value if no choice is available or if customers are reluctant or unable to shop around.

As a result, the audit approach to quality is still evolving. Auditors need to consider whether they can add to the information already produced by management and by consumer organisations or whether their role is best fulfilled by continuing to act as watch-dogs for consumers, citizens, taxpayers through their other VFM approaches.

Activity 4.2

Read the case study in Box 4.3, based on a report by the NAO. Try to examine the issues raised in the context of concepts discussed in the course.

This case gives an insight into the nature of the NAO's work. This example has been chosen since it covers key concepts from B821 in terms of differing valuation methods and transfer of risk, in this case from the public to the private sector. The timing of the sale is also of significance.

BOX 4.3   CASE STUDY: THE PRIVATISATION OF THE ROLLING STOCK LEASING COMPANIES

Sir John Bourn, head of the National Audit Office, reported to Parliament on the privatisation of the three rolling stock leasing companies (Angel, Eversholt and Porterbrook). The Department of Transport completed the sales in January and February 1996 to three separate purchasers for gross proceeds of £1.8 billion. By December 1997 all three businesses had been resold, each at a substantial profit. The then Government had seen major advantages in an early sale. Their over-riding objective in 1995 had been to secure the sale of the companies as soon as practicable. Sir John reported that the chosen timing of the sale probably had an adverse impact on proceeds. It affected the number of bidders and the prices they bid because:

- the identity of customers was not known at the time

- the businesses had little or no track record in the new rail industry

- bidders could not be certain that the overall rail privatisation programme would be completed because of political opposition to rail privatisation.

The Department commissioned a number of valuations of the companies in 1994. These initial valuations and ongoing discussions with bidders provided them with an insight into bidders' likely concerns and negotiating strategies. The Department did not update these valuations and did not carry out a comprehensive valuation. They believed at the time that this would not have been possible as no close private-sector comparators existed.

After the Department had received final bids and had selected preferred bidders they carried out an analysis of value. They concluded that bidders had adopted a cautious approach and that the bids were broadly consistent with each other. They also concluded that the bids were based on rates of return which seemed reasonable at the time, given uncertainty about how far the rail industry would be privatised. They were satisfied that the bids represented the best opportunity for achieving the key sale objectives.

The National Audit Office believed that it would have been possible to undertake a comprehensive valuation on the basis of an analysis of cash flows despite the absence of external comparators. They calculated that at the time of privatisation the value of the companies' future cash flows, under continuing public ownership, would have been £2.9 billion. The value obtained by the Government (sale proceeds, risks transferred and possible tax receipts) was up to £2.2 billion.

They also calculated the value of the businesses to the purchasers as between £2 billion, on very cautious assumptions, and £2.5 billion on more moderate (but not the most favourable) assumptions.

The Department do not accept the National Audit Office's analyses as being relevant because:

- they do not take account of the wider economic benefits which Ministers expected from the privatisation; and

- the over-riding objective was privatisation as soon as practicable.

In their view theoretical valuations would not have been useful and they consider that the value prospective purchasers actually placed on the companies, in the light of the risks perceived at the time, is ample evidence of this.

The Department attracted significant early interest in the sales. Nine bids were received at indicative bid stage, involving some 30 organisations. At the final bid stage there were only four bidders, resulting in two bids for each company. The Department succeeded in maintaining competitive tension between the final bidders.

The Department's objective from the outset was to sell the companies to three separate purchasers so as to encourage competition in the industry. They, therefore, sold Porterbrook for £55 million less than the highest bid, which was made by the winning bidders for Angel.

The Department made no provision to share in any gains made if the initial purchasers resold the companies. The National Audit Office found little written evidence of the Department considering this issue before final bids were received. The Department told the National Audit Office that they had considered, but decided against, including such provisions in the sale terms because of concern that such provisions would depress the price, deter bids and undermine competition in the sale.

For future sales of Government-owned assets or businesses the National Audit Office recommend that vendors should:

- carry out a valuation well ahead of bids to assist in negotiations with bidders and in deciding on the acceptability of bids

- give detailed and evidenced consideration as to the value for money achieved, and the reasons for proceeding, wherever the values of bids are low compared to analyses of value; and

- at an early stage, give detailed and evidenced consideration to the possibility of including provisions which allow them to share in gains made if businesses are resold.

The three rolling stock leasing companies have a total annual turnover of some £800 million in lease rentals from train operating companies. Part of the risk to the operating companies is restricted as eighty per cent of their income from initial leases (for periods up to 2004) is guaranteed by the Government.

Porterbrook management/employee buy-out consortium, whose main financial backers were Charterhouse, bought Porterbrook from the Department for £528 million in January 1996. In August 1996 they sold the business to Stagecoach Holdings for £826 million.

Eversholt management/employee buy-out consortium, whose main financial backers were the Candover Group and Electra Fleming, bought Eversholt from the Department for £518 million in February 1996. In February 1997 they sold the business to the Forward Trust Group for £726 million.

GRS Holding Company Limited, a consortium including Babcock and Brown and Nomura International, submitted bids for each rolling stock leasing company. They bought Angel from the Department in January 1996 for £696 million. GRS sold their right to Angel's capital rental income for some £690 million shortly after privatisation. In December 1997 they sold the remainder of the business to the Royal Bank of Scotland Group for £395 million. These transactions together valued Angel's business at some £1.1 billion, some 58% more than the Department had received.

In June 1997 the Department of Transport became part of the Department of the Environment, Transport and the Regions (DETR). In January 1998 they announced they had asked the Rail Regulator to report by April 1998 into the operation and possible regulation of the rolling stock leasing companies.

Source: NAO (1998)

The differences in the six approaches to VFM outlined above can be explained, in part, by the need to adjust to a variety of circumstances. However, it may also be due to the absence of general agreement about the purpose of VFM audit. If this is the case, then VFM auditing fails its own first principle of clarifying objectives. The analysis of the variety of approaches reveals that there is no consensus as to why VFM audits are undertaken, who they are for, or the methodology that should be employed.

Objectives of the audit range from providing information for public accountability through to helping management. In the USA, the General Accounting Office sees VFM auditing as providing information which is wanted and needed to hold government agencies accountable. Similarly, in the UK, the NAO carries out VFM audits predominantly for accountability purposes 'to provide parliament with independent information, assurance and advice about economy, efficiency and effectiveness'. By contrast, the Audit Commission interprets its main role as being to help management: 'to identify scope for improvements in economy, efficiency, and effectiveness and to use good practice as a lever to the not so good'.

The question of purpose is linked to the recipient of the report. The NAO reports to Parliament; by contrast the Audit Commission's national reports are for multiple audiences: central government, local authority members, local authority chief officers, professional bodies, the media and the general public. However, the VFM reports on individual local authorities are not available to the general public and are targeted primarily at chief officers and committee members. The target audience must influence the type of approach taken: if there is no mechanism for reinforcing the auditor's recommendations then the auditor must rely on persuading management.

Activity 4.3 _____

Consider how the various approaches to VFM audit could contribute towards better performance management in your organisation.

As with differences between public-sector organisations, the particular approach which would be most beneficial in your organisation would be contingent upon your own organisational circumstances. However, obtaining VFM can be applied as a measure in almost any organisation, for example support functions in commercial organisations.

4.2 THE FUTURE OF VALUE-FOR-MONEY AUDITING

The environment within which public-sector audit is operating has undergone significant changes and the precise role of audit in the changing public sector is far from clear. The recent changes increase the need for government auditors to address the questions raised above and pose additional questions such as whether VFM auditing should be increased or reduced, whether it requires better planning and co-ordination, whether more VFM audit should be contracted out and whether VFM audit can only be undertaken if it demonstrably 'adds value'. Where a programme is dependent on the performance of a number of agencies is the audit coverage sufficiently integrated? It is questionable how well the auditors work together to assess the impact of policies (Bowerman, 1994). It may be that VFM audit as we know it will be increasingly replaced by the broader concept of best value.

Best value will be covered in Section 4.3.

While the need for accountability has increased, the monitoring of some publicly funded bodies has reduced. In the UK, schools, the former polytechnics, colleges of further education, training and enterprise councils have all been removed from regular scrutiny by public-sector auditors. They have been replaced by private-sector auditors, often with no mandatory remit to review VFM and who work to different expectations of accountability. Their reports are to appointed boards or supervisory departments and not to Parliament or the public. While there is still limited scope for public sector auditors to undertake VFM work, this is made difficult, as they are not in routine contact with such bodies – there is a danger that an accountability gap may emerge.

The Audit Commission has highlighted the risk of reduced monitoring and warned of 'enormous' potential for waste in schools opted out of local authority control. Increasingly too, the audit bodies are required to compete for government audits. For example, in New Zealand almost 40% of government audit work is competitively tendered. The risk here is that the auditor is encouraged to regard the audited body, rather than the citizen, as the customer. As has happened in the private sector, this could lead to an unwillingness to upset the 'customer' for fear of losing the audit.

The emergence of competitive tendering for government audits and events such as the elimination of Auditor General's Office in California has encouraged scrutiny of the costs and benefits of VFM auditing. This has resulted in the audit bodies seeking to demonstrate 'added value', for example by showing that resultant savings will outweigh the cost of the audit. The NAO points out in its 1997 annual report that its investigations during the three years to 1997 led to £858m VFM savings. It also reminds readers that it adds value by making positive, constructive recommendations for improvement. Producing reports, which are useful to management, is therefore also an important dimension of value added.

There is a danger that if auditors concentrate solely on detecting savings and being helpful to managers that they may lose sight of some of their other functions and could impair independence. The NAO has been under pressure to abandon complex studies, particularly those on effectiveness, which are less likely to have a direct practical impact and therefore make demonstrating that they 'add value' difficult. Day and Klein (1990) describe the Audit Commission as 'a policeman constantly tempted to turn consultant'.

Policemen turned consultants?

4.3 BEST VALUE

Best value is a relatively new approach (which is likely to grow in importance through the life of this course). It combines audit with what management themselves should be doing. It is argued that the best value initiative encourages the adoption of a holistic and corporate approach, such that service delivery is not measured merely on cost (economy and efficiency) but also on quality.

So far in this section we have discussed how external audit has provided the impetus for improving strategic financial management in public-sector organisations. After more than fifteen years of operating in this capacity, the role of public-sector audit now seems set to become more focused along a combination of the 'audit of management representations' and 'comparative audit' models described above. This is in keeping with the principles of corporate governance enunciated by Cadbury (1992) and Nolan (1995) which emphasise that the responsibility for good financial management belongs to the organisation. Nevertheless in the absence of market forces and of a single success criterion, such as profitability, government is unwilling to leave good financial management solely to public bodies themselves. It is anxious to identify and rectify the failings of public-sector bodies. The auditor's role in all of this is still to be determined but is likely to take the form of verifying the validity and appropriateness of performance indicators reported by organisations and may extend to the auditor commenting on the overall strengths or weaknesses of the organisation based on reported performance. The auditors may have a further role in co-ordinating the work and findings of other 'inspectorates' which are also providing a commentary on the performance of the organisation. The most developed indication of this trend is the 'best value' initiative in UK local government, whereby a duty is to be placed on local authorities to obtain best value in the services they provide, in terms of both cost and quality (DETR, 1998a).

A system of performance indicators and targets will be central to this best value framework. A precise framework is yet to be fixed but, in outline, local authorities will be obliged to consult their local community in preparing an annual Local Performance Plan. This will include indicators of planned performance and will report on the previous year's performance against local and national targets. Local authorities will also be required to review all services on a 4–5 year rolling basis (i.e. 20–25% of budget each year). The main objective of these reviews will be to set (i) improved output targets in respect of economy, efficiency and effectiveness and (ii) an action plan to say how these improvements will be achieved. Indications so far are that audit/inspection will also play a prominent role in any best value regime.

BOX 4.4: BEST VALUE REVIEWS AND THE 4 C'S

Best value reviews are designed to be the principal way that new approaches to service delivery are considered. They are also intended to set demanding performance targets for all services so as to deliver continuous improvements. The framework for this is through the so-called 4 C's, that is to Challenge, Compare, Consult and Compete.

CHALLENGE

"to challenge the need for a service to be delivered at all"

COMPARE

"to compare the levels of service being provided against the best available, both inside and outside the public sector"

CONSULT

"to consult their local community, in order to give them a real voice in determining the quality and type of services which they pay for"

COMPETITION

"to ensure that services are competitive, in the sense that they bear comparison with the best and that, competition in what ever form, has been properly employed to bring about the continuous improvements in services that best value requires"

(Source: Adapted from DETR White paper, July 1998)

Key among the twelve principles of best value are:

- auditors should confirm the integrity and compatibility of performance information.
- auditors will report publicly on whether best value has been achieved and contribute to plans for remedial action (this will include agreeing measurable targets for improvement and reporting on progress against the agreed plan).
- there should be provision for intervention by the Secretary of State on Audit Commission advice to tackle failing councils.

It is significant that the terms 'audit' and 'inspection' are used together – the DETR (1998b) stresses that 'the skills of audit and inspection will be needed, acting in concert'. This is felt necessary because of the broad range of skills required under best value. The implication of this and the following statement is that external auditors are not good at making assessments of issues of quality:

> The Inspectorates bring a high degree of professional expertise to this task, and the government wishes to build on that in designing the best value framework. It takes the view that the independent external checks required under best value should aim to combine the best of both, audit

work – with its emphasis on efficiency and propriety – and inspection – with its emphasis on quality of service.

(DETR, 1998b)

Through best value, the auditors' efforts will be focused on the validity of performance indicators and the process by which they are set and will include certification to this effect in the Local Performance Plan. Best value, therefore, seems set to integrate the disparate aspects typified by the audit society: audit, inspection and performance measurement.

The importance of performance indicators must be stressed. They not only form part of some VFM approaches and are key to the best value approach. In addition, under resource accounting, government departments and agencies will have to set out their performance indicators, both financial and non-financial. Performance indicators are now crucial to both the public and private sectors.

SUMMARY

In this section we have examined financial management in the public sector, in particular how performance management can be exerted through value for money (VFM) auditing. Pressures on governments' finances have led to changes in the ways finances are managed. Many areas of the public sector have been put on to a more 'commercial' footing. It is unlikely that we have seen the end of these changes as the pressures for change will continue to exist. It seems likely that best value will increasingly replace VFM auditing, although the two are not incompatible. Of the six approaches to VFM, best value can be compared to the management representations audit and be seen as an extension of the comparative performance audit approach, with a more strategic point of view and fewer ad hoc investigations of waste.

5 PERFORMANCE MEASUREMENT AND INVESTMENT

5.1   Measurement of trustee performance   **58**

5.2   Measurement of fund manager performance   **63**

Summary   **70**

In this final section, we will look outside the organisation to investors and see how they, too, are subject to performance measurement. We also return to the theme of Section 1 of this unit, namely how institutional investors interact with managers and influence the choice of performance measures used throughout the organisations they invest in.

In the UK and USA, institutional investors play a major role in the investment scene. This is typical of countries in which governments have encouraged saving for later life via investment intermediaries, mainly through tax advantages. For example, in the UK, saving via a pension fund is tax deductible at the individual's marginal income tax rate; no tax is payable by the pension fund on gains made or income received; and tax is paid by the individual in later life on pensions received only after some allowance for tax-free lump sum payments.

Life assurance companies dominate what is known as the personal pension market where individuals save on their own account rather than through an occupational scheme.

This has led to pension funds and life assurance companies holding the majority of shares listed on the UK stock market. Individual investors, although keen buyers of privatisation shares during the 1980s, held only 20% of shares by value by 1994 compared with 67% in 1957. The switch to institutional investment has been less extreme in the USA, where individual investors have been encouraged to set up individual share portfolios as part of saving for retirement. This has led to a massive boom in individual ownership, with individual investors increasing in number from 7 million to 65 million in the period 1954 to 1998. However, institutional investors still control 40% by value of shares listed on the New York Stock Exchange.

5.1 MEASUREMENT OF TRUSTEE PERFORMANCE

Corporate pension funds in the UK operate under the trust system, where trustees are responsible for the stewardship of assets invested to meet current and future pensions of pension fund members. Legislation, such as the Pensions Act 1995, is designed to protect present and future pensioners by ensuring, for example, that the trustees represent the members' best interests and that pension funds are 'solvent' in the sense that they are likely to be able to pay out promised pensions. This is known as satisfying the **minimum funding requirement**. Trustees of corporate pension schemes are typically made up of a mixture of managers, employees and pensioners.

In a corporate pension scheme, the company (and usually employees as well) make contributions to a pension fund, and the monies paid in are invested in securities such as equities, bonds, property and cash deposits with a view to being used to pay out pensions as and when needed. Actuaries advise the trustees as to whether the pension fund is under- or over-funded depending on their expectations of the returns the securities invested in will generate and on the age and turnover profile of the workforce as well as the benefits promised. In terms of the returns the investments are supposed to generate, these will be based on a set of investment principles set out in the trust deed. This Statement of Investment Principles is now a requirement of the 1995 Pensions Act; an example of one such Statement is set out below in Table 5.1:

Table 5.1   Example of Trustee Statement of Investment Principles
(a) It should be the case that 'guaranteed benefits for each member can be paid from the scheme as they arise'.
(b) The solvency of the scheme on the Minimum Funding Requirement basis should be maintained.
(c) Subject to the preceding objectives, the aim should be to maximise the rate of returns earned on the assets over the long-term.

Source: Scott Bader Limited, Pension Fund Trust Deed, 1998

Notice how the requirements are specified in purely financial terms and exclude other issues which may be of relevance to trustees.

Activity 5.1

Suppose you are a trustee of the XYZ Foundation set up to promote research into science, which holds a large number of shares in XYZ, a pharmaceutical company, and that the shares have been underperforming the market over a long period. Should you as trustee sell most of the shares to achieve a better risk–return profile for the fund even if that makes the company vulnerable to take-over with the likelihood of redundancies?

This took place when Glaxo bid for Wellcome. The Wellcome Foundation had already sold off a large number of shares they held, not for lack of performance but because of the risk of holding too much in one share. This had made Wellcome vulnerable to approaches from other firms and jobs were indeed lost as a result of the merger with Glaxo.

Trustees have no expertise in the field of investment and are not expected to have any. Instead, they delegate the management of the pension fund assets either to an appointed fund manager employed by their company (**internal fund management**) or to a specialist **external fund management** company. The trend is towards external fund management, with many large funds, including the Universities Superannuation Scheme (in the top five largest pension funds in the UK) switching over to external fund management over the last few years. External fund managers bid for business from pension funds by making presentations to the trustees, and this process is popularly referred to as a 'beauty parade'. During this presentation, candidate fund management companies outline to the trustees their proposed investment strategy and their previous performance track record.

Perhaps these presentations are called beauty parades in deference to the economist, John Maynard Keynes, who famously referred to the process of choosing shares for investment portfolios as akin to choosing the winner in a beauty contest.

A beauty parade of pension fund managers?

One of the themes of B821 has been the link between return and risk. The higher the risk, the greater the return required by investors. We saw in Unit 1 how equities, with a greater standard deviation of returns than bonds, on average earn higher returns.

Given the pressures on trustees to earn high returns, evidenced by the last requirement in Table 5.1, should they allocate 100% of the investment funds for which they are responsible to equity investment? The risk inherent in such a strategy is that, during a particular three-month period, the return on the fund could be substantially negative and the trustees would have a lot of explaining to do. Trustees therefore prefer fund managers to put some of the funds into bonds and cash as well as equities, to diversify risk (using the precepts of portfolio theory described in Unit 4) and to reduce the risk of short-term loss.

This approach highlights the difficulty trustees have in deciding over what period of time they should aim, say, to maximise returns. Investment performance is typically measured every three months, with a detailed annual assessment, but pensions have long lives and employees may work for decades before needing a pension. A short-term focus on performance may cause trustees to take too much notice of volatility and push them towards a strategy less likely to achieve high returns in the long run.

It can be argued that corporate pension funds should be split into two parts: one part which is to pay pension liabilities already crystallised – for existing pensioners, and deferred pensions for employees who have left – and one part for the pensions of existing employees. With such a viewpoint, the first part should be invested in bonds and cash and the second part entirely in equities. This is because equities typically offer positive real returns in line with or greater than wage and salary increases. Only by investing in equities would the assets in the pension fund be able to keep up with the likely future pensions of current employees since these are typically based on final salaries. Such a split of assets would be following a **matching principle**, reducing risk in the way described in more detail in Unit 7.

This highlights a key issue of pension fund management. What should the objective be? In Table 5.1, it is expressed in terms of maximising returns but with requirements to limit the risk. It ignores non-financial issues and ignores the optimal time horizon. The answer from the trustee perspective should perhaps be some asset allocation optimisation process, using software such as PORT from Unit 4. This could include constraints designed to ensure matching where appropriate and to keep risk below prescribed levels, and the frequency of the data input into the model could be in line with the trustees' preferred time horizon.

However, fund managers, particularly external managers, may have a somewhat different objective function from that of trustees. Although they, too, want to achieve high returns without unacceptable risk, they are concerned with performance measurement, not with respect to the particular pension fund's future liabilities, but with respect to the performance of their peer group, who are other fund managers managing pension fund assets. Their objective is to be in the top quartile of the pension fund manager league tables in terms of quarterly performance. They are therefore reluctant to carry out a pure optimisation process which might lead to 'unusual' asset allocations, preferring to stick close to the median fund manager allocation. An example of this is given in Figure 5.1 which shows a fund manager's proposed typical maximum and minimum positions in each asset class relative to the benchmark which in this case, for a UK pension fund, they deem to be the WM All Funds index including property. This index is the median asset allocation for the 1,625 pension funds which provide information to WM, a UK performance measurement company.

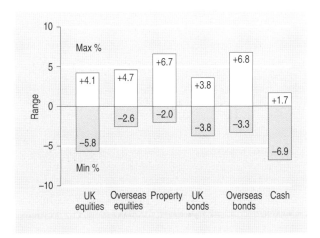

Figure 5.1   Fund manager's asset allocation strategy relative to the benchmark – min/max positions against benchmark (0) of WM All Funds, including property, 22 January 1991 to 31 December 1997 (Source: Morgan Grenfell Asset Management, 1998)

One interesting feature of the median asset allocation strategy of UK pension funds is how different it is from what financial theory would predict. Figure 5.2 shows the equity allocation strategy for *non-UK* equities as of April 1998 of the median UK pension fund as measured by another consulting firm, CAPS. Figure 5.2 also includes the equity allocation strategy recommended by the capital asset pricing model or CAPM (described in Unit 4 and in *Vital Statistics*).

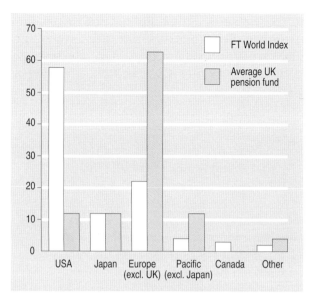

Figure 5.2 Possible equity allocation strategies (Source: Barclays Global Investors, 1998)

One implication of the CAPM is that, if investors have no prior expectations, they should follow a passive investment strategy and invest in equities in proportion to their market size. Although the CAPM is difficult to extend theoretically to an international framework, common sense would suggest that a passive approach would also be appropriate for the unskilled investor when investing in global equity markets. Following such a strategy for non-UK equities in 1998 would have meant investing 57% of an equity portfolio in the US stock market, 22% in Europe, excluding the UK, and 11% in Japan. However, the median fund strategy is very different from the passive approach. First, fund managers invest in non-domestic markets in weights very different from those which market values would suggest. For example, from Figure 5.2, we can see that their active strategy involves being substantially underweight in the US market and overweight in Europe. Such an active strategy would clearly lead to massive under- or over-performance relative to a market-weighted index, but the fund manager, if judged relative to the CAPS index, would achieve results close to the median. Second, they tend to have a much higher percentage of the portfolios they manage invested in the home market, in this case, the UK. This is because UK pension fund liabilities are in sterling and also, perhaps, because UK fund managers perceive the domestic market as having lower risk since they believe they understand it better!

However, many UK companies earn profits abroad and may not, as we saw in Unit 8, hedge all their exchange risk, so investing in UK equities can be an indirect way of investing overseas.

This makes the trustees' decision very difficult. Should they follow the academic theories and put their money in the largest markets or should they follow the herd and simply try to match or beat the average fund manager? Suppose the CAPM-dictated strategy failed to deliver in any one quarter and the fund was in the bottom quartile? The trustees would be in breach of their investment principles. On the other hand, coming in with average performance can cause no such reproaches. As a result, with the appointment of trustees, most UK fund managers adopted the equity allocation approach outlined in Figure 5.2 throughout the 1990s and failed to take advantage of the massive rise in US equities over that time.

One more dilemma for the trustees. Some pension funds, notably UK local authority funds, adopt an ethical stance to investment – choosing to exclude armament companies, tobacco companies and firms with interests in gambling from the possible investments. This may also cause under-performance relative to an unconstrained benchmark. If the Statement of Investment Principles does not clearly adjust the appropriate benchmark to take account of ethical constraints, the trustees of the pension fund of an ethical organisation might well be reproached for not investing in unethical activities!

Activity 5.2 _____

What are the Investment Principles underlying your organisational pension fund scheme and what is the benchmark used to judge investment performance?

5.2   MEASUREMENT OF FUND MANAGER PERFORMANCE

Suppose now that a fund manager has been appointed and that the trustees are happy to judge the fund manager by his or her performance relative to the median pension fund's performance. How will the fund manager go about trying to achieve outperformance? (Remember that he or she has to earn something on top of the benchmark return to cover the likely fees which are around 50 basis points or ½% for up to £50m of assets for an actively managed fund.)

There are two ways that fund managers can try to outperform – one is through a better **asset allocation** than the median fund manager achieves and the other is through better **stock selection** than the peer group benchmark. In the case of asset allocation, this would mean being overweight in markets and types of security which do relatively well over the required time horizon, say three months or a year, and underweight in those that do relatively badly. Stock selection means being overweight in shares or bonds expected to do well and underweight in poorly performing shares or bonds, in both cases the performance being judged relative to a bond index.

On the whole, fund managers are poor at asset allocation. We have seen how fund managers in the 1990s failed to predict the meteoric rise of the US stock markets and were over-optimistic about Japan. This led them to underperform the market value weighted global equity index by around 10% per annum throughout this period. However, most fund managers pride themselves on their stock selection skills, that is the ability to pick shares which will outperform a domestic index. In the case of UK pension funds, the benchmark UK equity index could, for example, be the FT-SE All-Share Index.

See Unit 4, Section 2.2, for a brief description of the FT-SE All-Share Index.

Each fund management company has a different investment process for choosing in which shares to be overweight and in which shares to be underweight. These will involve the use of some or all of the following:

- technical analysis such as studying charts or devising trading rules based on share price patterns
- fundamental analysis such as company analysis, market ratio analysis, industry analysis, or economic analysis, as discussed in Block 2 and in Unit 6
- key information gleaned from company visits and perhaps not publicly available.

"Wait a moment – make that sell."

There are strict rules on what information may be passed on to equity analysts or fund managers during company visits or presentations. However, it is likely that analysts studying companies in depth will have access, not to insider information, but to insights not available to the ordinary individual investor.

In Unit 1, we introduced the concept of the efficient markets hypothesis (EMH) and the three types of analysis described above each tie in with a level of the EMH – weak, semi-strong and strong. Active managers, by definition, must believe that markets are inefficient at one level or another or they would not believe that they could – consistently – outperform.

No fund manager will divulge the full details of the investment process they go through to select shares but each will tell you that they have a consistent process, with key investment themes and, most importantly, a strict risk-management process. Most fund managers nowadays use some version of portfolio theory, the CAPM or a more complete multi-factor model to manage the risk of their portfolios and to try to outperform a benchmark within pre-specified risk constraints. For example, they will say that they are likely (but not guaranteed!) to achieve on average a 1% annualised outperformance for a tracking error of 1% or a 3 to 4% annualised outperformance for a 5% tracking error, where **tracking error** means the difference between the risk (measured by standard deviation of returns) of their portfolio and the risk of the benchmark portfolio. Using computers to analyse the risk of portfolios and to develop a consistent investment process is becoming more common.

Activity 5.3

Listen again to Audio 1, 'Fund management', which you first heard when studying Unit 4. This time, listen to how computers and financial models are used to develop a rigorous investment process which is attractive to pension fund clients.

Whatever the investment process, there are certain key numbers which fund managers look at with respect to the companies they analyse and these are the numbers you studied in Blocks 2 and 3. Accounting ratios such as ROCE and profit margins are key as are PE ratios, EV/EBITDA and price to book value. Given the relative nature of the investment process, fund managers are looking for shares which are relatively cheap or dear and will look at their ratios relative to the sector, the market or the benchmark.

Fund managers are keen to achieve a good track record, that is to be able to show above average performance over a number of years to potential clients. You will not be surprised to learn that each potential fund manager varies the way in which he or she presents performance statistics, to put them in the best possible light. More objective evidence from performance measurement consultants such as WM and CAPS shows that fund managers rarely exceed an index benchmark for a particular market and, if they do, this performance is unlikely to last more than a few years. This is even more the case once fund management fees for active management are taken into account and this failure to add value is now influencing both pension fund trustees and individual investors' investment strategy.

> There is no evidence that fund managers can deliver above average performance, and every reason to believe that the average consumer would be better off with a passively managed fund.

Source: Recent OFT report

Investment managers' prize-giving ceremony

Many trustees are switching to a passive (index fund) investment strategy for their funds, away from the active strategy favoured by most fund managers. Over $1,400bn of pension fund assets in the USA, and £130bn of UK pension fund assets, were managed passively in 1998 (HSBC Securities, 1998). With the UK government 'kitemarking' index funds for individual pension savings, the amount of money under passive management is likely to grow. The pressure on fund managers to add value is at least as intense as on corporate managers.

BOX 5.1   TRACKERS TRIP UP THE TOP PENSION FUNDS

The big four, Gartmore, Schroders, PDFM and MAM, who between them manage 60 per cent of Britain's pension funds, are in crisis. Their style of investment management, which relies on the skills of their fund managers to decide which shares to buy and in what industries, is looking increasingly old fashioned and ineffective.

Clients are becoming restive: already, unprecedented numbers have switched to other managers, and many others are considering following suit. And the pension consultants, hitherto great fans of the balanced approach, are calling for dramatic changes.

Funds which replace expert human judgment with sophisticated computer techniques to track the performance of any index from the FT All Share to Australian Small Companies, are winning unprecedented amounts of business.

More than £13 billion flowed into Barclays Global Investors and Legal & General, the two market leaders, last year. BGI has added £2bn more already this year, and is budgeting for £9bn by the end of the year.

Tracking, or indexation, is already big business in the US: about a quarter of pension funds there use it, and some estimate that 40 per cent of all institutional investment is in some form of tracker fund. Here, however, pension fund trustees have clung to the idea that active management brings better performance.

The figures suggest it can – but not in the way that the managers would hope: figures from WM Company, which analyses pension performance, show actively managed funds underperforming the All-Share index in six of the past 10 years, even before fees are taken into account.

What makes the case for indexation all the more compelling is that tracker funds charge between 0.07 per cent and 0.1 per cent – roughly half what balanced managers charge. This is fine when markets are rising, but what happens when indexation merely means tracking a falling market?

Lindsay Tomlinson, chief executive of BGI, does not think that would matter. 'That would be an argument about asset allocation [that is, which category of investments funds to put the money into], rather than stock selection. You could be indexed and still have lots of cash.'

He thinks there is more room for substantially more growth in indexation. 'The Pensions Act and the Minimum Funding Requirement [which could force some funds to reduce their equity holdings], maturing pension funds and so on, mean funds need a different structure. The decision to employ a specialist, including an index specialist, therefore becomes much easier.'

Trackers are not the only funds that are doing well. US investment houses such as JP Morgan, Capital International and Fidelity, whose investment processes are so rigid that they have more in common with index funds than balanced managers, are also winning large amounts of business.

'We use a lot of judgment and insight, but also a lot of maths,' said the head of one such firm. 'We remove as much risk as possible. We also try not to do the things we know we are not good at – sector allocation for example. You can't consistently call whether drugs and banks are going to be better performers than retail stores. So what we do is decide our country and currency allocations.

'Then when we go into, say, France, we have the same weight in each sector as the market. But we have robust stock selection, based on detailed research of companies, because that is where we think we can add value.'

This is increasingly what the consultants want. William Mercer has for years been advising clients to choose a range of specialists. 'It is logical,' says Tim Gardener, a consultant actuary with the firm. 'If you consider the US market, for example, there are 15,000 fund managers, some of them huge. How can you expect a UK fund manager with five people to make better US investments than they can?'

He is particularly critical of the balanced fund managers' skills in deciding which country or sector to put their money in. 'There is almost no occasion on which the balanced fund managers have got the buy and sell decisions right. For example, the big fund managers got the buy decision on the Pacific Basin right in the late Eighties. But they should have got rid of them a year ago, when the market had risen by 100 per cent in a year. They did not, and all the value that was added from being in early has been lost.'

Source: The Observer, 5 April 1998

Measurement of management performance

We have already discussed how fund managers tend to invest in companies at arm's length and have been accused of merely voting with their feet when managers underperform rather than using their votes or even their personal influence to effect organisational change. It has been argued that the market for corporate control, discussed in Section 2, would not be necessary if pension fund and other institutional fund managers took their role as investors more seriously.

A number of high-profile pension funds in the US, most notably CALpers, the pension fund of California's state employees, have begun to flex their muscles and use their vote more aggressively and some movement has been made in the UK towards this. Fund managers (and the analysts who sell them ideas) have privileged access to management in the sense that directors make presentations to fund managers, talk to them regularly on the telephone and welcome visits to company headquarters and other sites. Fund managers can also influence such decisions as choice of chief executive, chair, non-executive directors and remuneration policy for executives.

Some progress has been made on voting strategy by institutional investors. Most are encouraged to cast their own vote at corporate Annual General Meetings or Extraordinary General Meetings rather than adopting the more passive approach of allowing their votes to be cast as the directors see fit. This passive approach to voting has allowed senior managers of firms with substantial institutional investor holdings, for example those firms in the FT-SE 100, to act as they see fit and to fight off any criticism by small investors, whose holdings are insufficient to make an impact on any vote.

Institutional investors have also become involved in discussions over executive pay, in particular schemes where pay is linked to performance. They have encouraged schemes such as that implemented at BP which is designed to achieve just the level of outperformance relative to a benchmark which they as fund managers need to achieve (see Box 5.2).

> ### BOX 5.2   BP LONG-TERM PERFORMANCE PLAN – EXTRACT FROM THE REMUNERATION COMMITTEE REPORT, BP ANNUAL REPORT AND ACCOUNTS, 1997
>
> 'The primary performance measure for the Plan is BP's total shareholder return in relation to a chosen peer group of seven major oil companies (Amoco, Arco, Chevron, Exxon, Mobil, Shell Transport and Trading, and Texaco). This measure of total shareholder return eliminates the differential growth elements attributable to movements in UK and US markets. Participants benefit only when they deliver hard business results that benefit shareholders.
>
> For example, the maximum award may be made only when BP's performance exceeds all the selected competitors and performance is also satisfactory against the secondary measures of trends in cash flow, return on capital employed, earnings per share and the absolute magnitude of BP's shareholder return ... No award will be made to directors if BP's performance is below the median of selected competitors.'

However, there is clearly some way still to go as the FT survey described in Box 5.3 highlights:

BOX 5.3   SHARES IN THE ACTION

An FT survey asks what part leading shareholders play in the running of companies and what top directors think of their investors.

Table 5.2   What finance directors think of their shareholders

How often do your major investors try to use muscle behind the scenes to make you change your strategy, financial targets or corporate governance?

Occasionally	Rarely	Never	N/A
7%	51%	41%	1%

Do you feel hampered in taking the correct long-term strategy?

Yes	No	N/A
7%	89%	4%

How often do your major investors make useful comments about your business?

All the time	Often	Occasionally	Rarely	Never	N/A
1%	7%	43%	45%	3%	1%

How well do your major investors understand your business?

Very well	Quite well	Well	Poorly
13%	29%	56%	1%

Has your major investors' involvement over the issue of executive pay been:

Very helpful?	Helpful?	Neutral?	Unhelpful?	N/A?
1%	24%	57%	3%	15%

Do you feel major investors are long-term investors?

Yes	No	N/A
98%	1%	1%

How do shareholders actually affect the running of UK businesses? And what do directors of the UK's 100 biggest companies really think of the institutional investors who own their assets?

The answers, in a no-holds barred survey carried out by the FT, make salutary reading for those who see the Anglo-Saxon model of share ownership as the brave new world order.

Under this vision, well-informed shareholders take an active role in improving company performance; they keep executives on their toes by asking awkward questions about strategy; they punish mistakes by disinvesting; and they reward good performance by bidding up the share price, making it easier or cheaper for companies to raise more money.

The reality, as seen through the eyes of the company directors involved, is a little more prosaic. While there is widespread evidence that fund managers are demanding more interviews, the usefulness of meetings is often questioned by finance directors called to them. Many of the 74 finance directors interviewed for the survey resented the time spent educating fund managers who are moved on before gaining adequate knowledge.

Several directors were also irked by fund managers who ask for more and more attention. 'When they want a meeting they want it now, which is very frustrating when you are trying to run a business,' said one.

Some of the comments will leave their unidentified speakers open to charges of thinking like corporate dinosaurs. 'Some [institutional investors] believe that they own the business,' said one director. 'But they are traders in financial instruments.' That comment ignores the most basic tenet of the Anglo-Saxon view of capitalism: shareholders *do* own the business.

A more common criticism of shareholders is that they rarely add anything that the companies perceive to be of value. Almost half of those surveyed felt that their main shareholders 'rarely or never' offered any useful comments about their business.

A surprising number of directors expressed the view that shareholders were too docile a breed in general. 'We often wonder why institutional investors tolerate inadequate performance in other companies,' said one director. 'They could often be tougher. We sometimes wish shareholders would *be* tougher.'

It is often said that the increasing globalisation of investment habits makes for a tougher environment for companies. But one notable feature of the survey was the dominance of a handful of UK fund management companies. When asked to single out companies for praise or criticism, more directors mentioned Mercury, the Prudential and Schroder – the three largest UK managers – than any other. They were particularly praised for their understanding of the business.

The popularity of these managers possibly relates to their size. Citywatch, the market research company, estimates that the top five fund managers own 26 per cent of the FTSE 100, while the top 10 have 36 per cent, a far greater concentration than is found in the US market. In these circumstances, few fund managers can afford to move out of a FTSE 100 company altogether and therefore remain long-term shareholders whether the investment is liked or not.

Such concentration also makes it easy to see why directors are prepared to spend the time on one-to-one meetings with their largest managers while they can resent the behaviour of the smaller shareholders who 'lack understanding'.

The concentration of ownership could also help explain one of the most surprising results of the survey: company directors disagree with the widely held view among corporate governance groups and government officials that shareholders are short-termist. Almost all directors felt their biggest shareholders were in it for the long term. This provides an important corrective to the view that the City damages companies by forcing them to abandon long-term projects for the sake of quick returns.

The survey also cast doubt on the claim often put forward by fund managers that they work behind the scenes to deal with issues of corporate governance. Perhaps surprisingly, almost all of the directors interviewed – 92 per cent – said that shareholders rarely or never tried to use their muscle to make changes behind the scenes.

Of course directors and executives do not necessarily give an impartial account of the role of shareholders. So, while a fifth of all directors admitted to having had a serious disagreement with their leading shareholders over the past five years, this may understate the situation.

Whatever the facts on behind-the-scenes behaviour, some directors were irritated by off-the-record briefings to journalists by fund managers. Investors claim to use these briefings when all other avenues are closed. One director fumed: 'I don't think the FT should quote an anonymous shareholder saying I am useless. They should be prepared to stand up and be counted.'

The behaviour of UK investors contrasts sharply with that of their rivals across the Atlantic.

'US investors are more concerned to understand the business and want to meet people who run the individual divisions,' said one finance director. 'They are less satisfied with the odd chat with the chief executive and finance director.'

US managers – notably Capital International and Fidelity, which have both roughly doubled their UK equity exposure in the past five years – won plaudits for working harder on meetings and employing more in-house analysts.

However, there was evidence of some unease with the increasing familiarity. 'The US managers look for more intimate relationships. They try to understand what it's like to be you. This is not bad, but you have to learn to handle it. It can be stressful,' said one director.

Some directors were more seriously uncomfortable about particularly probing questions. 'The Americans will try to get price-sensitive information out of you and they get annoyed if they don't secure it,' said one.

However, several directors felt that UK fund management was becoming more Americanised and that communication was improving as a result. 'The UK will inevitably move more to a US approach and that's not a bad thing,' said one director of a multinational company. Continental European investors were rarely mentioned and, when they were, comments were negative.

The influence of US investors, who are conservatively estimated to have a 10 per cent stake in the UK market, appears to have had a far greater impact than the first two corporate governance reports produced by top-level committees of City professionals and industrialists.

Some 81 per cent of directors said that the Cadbury and Greenbury codes on corporate governance produced since 1993 had had no effect on their relationship with their investors.

One director was moved to say: 'I am surprised at the lack of interest in Cadbury and Greenbury among major shareholders. It's never discussed at meetings with them. I would welcome greater involvement on the additional reporting requirements.'

Fund mangers did not come out well on the issue of voting on company issues, for example at annual meetings. Institutional investors often claim that they vote on virtually every issue. Yet just 3 per cent of directors believed their shareholders voted every time, while another 47 per cent believed they voted on 'most occasions'.

These figures are likely to add grist to the mill of the UK government, which has put the fund management industry on notice that it will be forced to vote if it does not improve its record.

Companies claimed they also received little feedback about how those votes were cast, with 49 per cent saying that shareholders only occasionally explained their decisions.

In spite of the problems, the relationship between the UK's largest companies and their principal shareholders does appear to have improved. Factors may include increased political and public interest in corporate governance or greater competition.

Some 68 per cent of companies said they were happy with their relationship, while 23 per cent said they were very happy and 9 per cent said they were satisfied.

Desultory questioning of executives, for example over strawberries in the corporate hospitality tent at Wimbledon, does appear to have been replaced with far greater analysis, often to the discomfort of the companies concerned. 'They are more professional and better researched than five years ago,' admitted one director.

Few of those involved, whether finance directors or shareholders, believe that the trend towards greater involvement and communication between the two sides is going to end. This is partly because of increased US investment and partly because of the threat of government intervention. 'Investors are much more sensitive to their responsibilities than in the past because they are looked on as the guardians of the corporate conscience,' said one director. 'And that's much better than the government doing it.'

The poll comprising companies in the FTSE 100 index was conducted by FT journalists with finance directors and in a few cases, with other relevant senior executives. There was a 74 per cent response rate.

Source: Financial Times, *27 April 1998*

Activity 5.4

Listen to Audio 6, 'Corporate governance', which features BP and Scott Bader, two very different UK-based companies which you have already come across in this unit. Listen for differences between the two companies on perceptions of stakeholders, performance measures, executive remuneration and motivation.

SUMMARY

In this section, we have looked at the world of institutional investment from a different perspective. We have seen how pension fund trustees are also subject to their own performance measures, a complex business given how difficult it is to specify financial objectives for pension funds when compared with specifying financial objectives for companies. We then looked at fund managers and how they are judged on performance relative to their peers rather than a market-value-weighted index and how this can lead to underperformance by all fund managers. Finally, we returned to the topic of Section 2, corporate governance, and saw how pressure on institutional investors to perform has led to pressure on senior and divisional managers to introduce value-based performance measures and value-related incentive schemes.

SUMMARY AND CONCLUSIONS

In this concluding unit, we have attempted to integrate a number of themes from the course as a whole, in particular finance and accounting. We have looked at how accounting and finance are used to control behaviour – of senior managers by outside investors (namely the corporate governance issue), and of middle managers by senior managers – through performance measures, both in the public and private sectors.

In Section 2, we looked at corporate governance issues in more detail than we had done in Unit 1 and considered the two main methods of corporate governance: market-based, as practised in the USA and the UK; and relationship-based, as practised, until recently, in Japan, Germany and France. The advantages and disadvantages of each method were noted, as was the global trend towards market-based corporate governance.

In Section 3, we looked in more depth than in Unit 1 at the roles of internal and external reporting, namely management and financial accounting, in terms of their functions. We identified three main functions for management accounting: planning, decision-making and control; and three main functions for financial accounting: decision-making, stewardship and accountability.

We looked at how concentration on control mechanisms is gradually being replaced by performance measures, and how performance measures imposed from outside the organisation are being imposed within the organisation on divisional managers. Examples of such performance measures include CFROI, ROIC and EVA. Such performance measures are related to economic rather than accounting income but typically use accounting surrogates for cash flow returns.

Section 4 turned attention to the public sector where similar trends can be identified. Performance measurement of outputs is becoming more prevalent than control of inputs. The role of auditing in the public sector is changing to reflect this and the section outlined six stages in the evolution of value for money auditing:

1   review of management systems, arrangements and procedures

2   value for money procedures audit

3   policy audit

4   audit of management representations of value for money

5   comparative performance audit

6   quality audit.

The section also included a case study of an investigation into the government sale of the UK rolling stock leasing companies.

The final section, Section 5, looked at the role of performance measurement in investment, going back to look at how the institutional investors, who measure the performance of companies, are themselves measured. The measurement of pension fund trustee performance is one such example and, by the end of this section, several difficulties in choosing an appropriate asset allocation and risk/return strategy were identified. The section concluded by coming full circle to see how managers perceive the institutional investors who are effectively owners of their companies.

You should now have achieved the following learning objectives and be able to:

- assess the relevance and relative efficiency of different structures of corporate governance
- describe how external investment managers and internal line managers assess the performance of different investments and operating units respectively
- show how performance measures such as economic value added, cash flow return on investment and discounted cash flow analysis can be used both as external and as internal performance measures
- apply the principles of value-for-money auditing in the context of the public sector
- describe the financial objectives and performance measures used by institutional investors such as pension funds.

ANSWERS TO EXERCISES

Exercise 2.1

A: Boots

B: Scott Bader

C: BP

D: Daimler-Benz

Notice how there is little difference between the three UK companies although it is clear that Daimler-Benz, at the time of writing, had not yet come round fully to the shareholder perspective, as we showed in Unit 1.

Exercise 3.1

The effect of a reduced WACC would be an increased EVA, provided returns were not also affected. Given that senior managers do not influence the level of interest rates, it could be argued that they should not be rewarded for increases in EVA due to such a change.

Exercise 3.2

The operating lease payments may represent, say, 5% of the capital value of the properties. Adding back operating lease rentals to NOPAT and capitalising the operating leases as part of invested capital will substantially reduce EVA. However, Boots can be considered as part property company and part retailer and it might be more appropriate to judge each activity separately using a different WACC in each case.

REFERENCES

Audit Commission (1991) *How Effective is the Audit Commission?* Audit Commission, London.

Auditor General of Canada (1992) *Report of the Auditor General of Canada to the House of Commons 1992*, Ottawa, Canada.

Berle, A. and Means G.C. (1932) *The Modern Corporation and Private Property*, Macmillan, New York.

Bowerman, M. (1994) 'The National Audit Office and the Audit Commission: co-operation in areas where their VFM responsibilities interface', *Financial Accountability and Management*, Vol. 10, No. 1, pp. 47–64.

Bowerman, M. (1995) 'Auditing performance indicators: the role of the Audit Commission in the citizen's charter initiative', *Financial Accountability and Management*, Vol. 11, No. 2, pp. 171–84.

Bowerman, M. (1996) 'The rise and fall of value for money auditing', in I. Lapsley and F. Mitchell (eds), *Accounting and Performance Measurement Issues in the Private and Public Sectors*, Paul Chapman Press.

Bradley, M., Desai, A. and Kim, E.H. (1988) 'Synergistic gains from corporate acquisitions and their division between the stockholders of target and acquiring firms', *Journal of Financial Economics*, Vol. 21, No. 1, pp. 3–40.

Cadbury, A. (1992) *Report of the Committee on the Financial Aspects of Corporate Governance*, London, Gee.

Canadian Comprehensive Auditing Foundation (1987) *Effectiveness Reporting and Auditing In The Public Sector*, CCAF, Ottawa, Canada.

Carr, R. (1996) 'Towards a truer measure of value,' *Financial Times*, 11 December.

Chew, D. (1997) *Studies in International Corporate Finance and Government Systems, a comparison of the US, Japan and Europe*, Oxford University Press.

Chisman, N. (1998) 'Why I support the Statement of Principles', *Financial Reporting Today – Current and Emerging Issues*, Accountancy Books.

Coote, A. (1994) 'Performance and quality in public services', in A. Conner and S. Black (eds), *Performance Review And Quality In Social Care*, Jessica Kingsley Publishers, London.

Day, P. and Klein, R. (1990) *Inspecting the Inspectorates*, Joseph Rowntree Memorial Trust.

Demsetz, H. and Lehn, K. (1985) 'The structure of corporate ownership: causes and consequences', *Journal of Political Economy*, Vol. 93, pp. 1155–77.

DETR (1998a) 'Modernising local government – improving local services through best value', DETR, 1998-04-23.

DETR (1998b) 'Best value update – issue two', April, DETR.

Dewar, D. (1989) 'Value for money audit in the National Audit Office', *Internal Auditing*, October, pp. 2–5.

Dillon R.D. and Owers, J.E. (1997) 'EVA as a financial metric: attributes, utilization, and relationship to NPV', *Financial Practice and Education*, Spring/Summer, pp. 32–54.

Donaldson, G. (1961) 'Corporate debt capacity', Division of Research, Graduate School of Business Administration, Harvard University, Boston.

Francis, G.A.J., Hinton, C.M., Holloway, J. and Mayle, D. (1998) 'A role for management accountants in best practice benchmarking?', Open University Business School Working Paper, 98/2.

Franks, J. and Mayer, C. (1997) 'Corporate ownership and control in the UK, Germany and France', *Journal of Applied Corporate Finance*, Vol. 9, No. 4, pp. 30–45.

General Accounting Office (1988) *Standards for Audit of Government Programs Activities and Functions*, US General Accounting Office.

Gilson, S.C. and Vetsuypens, M.R. (1993) 'CEO compensation in financially distressed firms: an empirical analysis', *Journal of Finance*, Vol. 48, pp. 425–58.

HM Treasury (1995) *Better Accounting for the Taxpayer's Money: resources accounting and budgeting in government*, White Paper Cm 2929.

HSBC Securities (1998) *Fund Management, Major Themes*, June.

Hutton, W. (1995) *The State We're In*, Jonathan Cape.

INTOSAI/United Nations (1977) *Public Sector Audit Standards*, United Nations Secretariat, New York.

Jensen, M.C. (1991) 'Corporate control and the politics of finance', *Journal of Applied Corporate Finance*, Vol. 4, pp. 13–33.

Jensen, M.C. and Meckling, W.C. (1976) 'Theory of the firm: managerial behavior, agency costs and capital structure', *Journal of Financial Economics*, Vol. 3, pp.305–60.

Jensen, M.C. and Murphy, K.J. (1998) 'Performance pay and top management incentives', *Journal of Political Economy*, Vol. 98, pp. 225–63.

Kaplan, S.N. (1997) 'Corporate governance and corporate performance: a comparison of Germany, Japan and the US', *Journal of Applied Corporate Finance*, Vol. 9, No.4, pp. 86–93.

Local Government Chronicle (1997) 'Armstrong unveils best value blueprint', 6 June, pp. 1, 3.

Magill, J. (1994) *Statement by Mr John Magill the Appointed Auditor for Westminster City Council*, Touche Ross & Co., London.

Murphy, K.J. (1985) 'Corporate performance and managerial remuneration: an empirical analysis', *Journal of Accounting and Economics*, Vol. 7, pp. 11–42.

National Audit Office (1992) *The Sale of the Twelve Regional Electricity Companies*, HC10 (1992/3), HMSO London.

National Audit Office (1993) *Annual Report 1993*, NAO, London.

National Audit Office (1997) *Annual Report* 1997, NAO, London.

National Audit Office (1998) NAO Press Notice 23/98 *Report by the Comptroller and Auditor General,* HC 576 1997/98, 5 March.

National Audit Office (1991) *Helping The Nation Spend Wisely,* NAO, London.

Normanton, E.L. (1966) *The Accountability and Audit of Governments,* Manchester University Press.

Ohlson, J. (1989) 'Accounting earnings, book value and dividends: the theory of the clean surplus equation (Part I)', in R. Brief and K. Peasnell (eds) *Clean Surplus: A Link between Accounting and Finance,* New York, Garland.

Ohlson, J. (1995) 'Earnings, book values, and dividends in equity valuation', *Contemporary Accounting Research,* Spring, pp. 661–87.

O'Hanlon, J. and Peasnall, K. (1998) 'Wall Street's contribution to management accounting: the Stern Stewart EVA financial management system', Working Paper, Management School, Lancaster University.

Pallot J. (1992) Local authority reporting: major advances made', *Accountants' Journal of the New Zealand Society of Accountants* Wellington NZ, August, pp. 46–9.

Pallot J. and Ball, I. (1997) 'What difference does resource accounting make, the case of New Zealand', *Public Expenditure Effective Management,* ed. D. Corry, Dryden Press. pp. 237–52.

Pallot, J. (1991) 'Accounting, auditing and accountability', in Boston (ed.) *Reshaping The State,* pp. 198–232.

Power, M. (1994) *The Audit Explosion,* DEMOS paper No. 7.

Preinreich, G. (1938) 'Annual study of economic theory: the theory of depreciation', *Econometrica,* July, pp. 219–41.

Radford, M. (1991) 'Auditing for change: local government and the Audit Commission', *Modern Law Review,* Vol. 54, No. 6, pp. 912–32.

Ryan, H.E., and Trahan, E.A. (1997) 'Utilizing value-based management systems to maximize shareholder value: a survey of CFOs', Northeastern University Working Paper.

Sharkansky, I. (1991) 'The auditor as policy maker', in A. Friedberg, B. Geist, N. Mizrahi and I. Sharkansky (eds) *State Audit and Accountability: a Book of Readings,* State of Israel, State Comptroller's Office, Jerusalem, pp. 74–94.

Spencer, C. and Francis, G.A.J. (1998) 'Divisional performance measures: economic value added as a proxy for shareholder wealth', Proceedings of Performance Management Theory and Practice Conference, Cambridge 1998.

Stern, J., Stewart, G. and Chew, D. 'The EVA® financial management system', *Journal of Applied Corporate Finance,* Summer, pp. 32–46.

Swedish Ministry of Finance Budget Department (1995) *Annual Performance Accounting and Auditing in Sweden,* Stockholm.

The Nolan Committee (1995) *Standards in Public Life,* Vol. 1, Cm 2850-1.

Zimmerman, J.L. (1997) 'EVA and divisional performance measurement: capturing synergies and other issues', *Journal of Applied Corporate Finance,* Vol. 10, No. 2, pp. 98–109.

ACKNOWLEDGEMENTS

Grateful acknowledgement is made to the following sources for permission to reproduce material in this unit:

Illustrations

p. 6: © BBC Picture Archives; p. 12: © Martin Rowson; pp. 13, 19: Reprinted with permission from the creators from Stocksworth: An American CEO, 1998; p. 25: Roger Beale, from the *Financial Times*; p. 28: Reproduced from *Bookmark*, March 1999, by kind permission of the Chartered Institute of Management Accountants; pp. 41, 55, 60: © The Hulton Getty Picture Collection; p. 45: Eastern Group plc; p. 47: © House of Commons Education Unit; p. 49: © Ted Goff www.tedgoff.com ; p. 61: © Chris Duggan; *Figure 5.1:* Scott Bader Co. Ltd Retirement Benefit Scheme, Nick Baulsch and Richard Dyson, April 1998 by permission of Morgan Grenfell Investment Management Limited; *Figure 5.2:* Barclays Global Investors, 1998; p. 64: Mik Jago; p. 65 (top): © Geoff Thompson, *Sunday Times*.

Tables

Table 2.1: Kaplan, S.N. (1997) 'Corporate governance and corporate performance', *Journal of Applied Corporate Finance*, Vol. 9, No. 4, winter 1997, Stern Stewart Management Services; *Table 4.1:* reprinted by permission of Paul Chapman Publishing from Bowerman, M. (1996) 'The rise and fall of value for money auditing', in *Accounting and Performance Measurement*, Lapsley, I. and Mitchell, F. Copyright © 1996 Irvine Lapsley and Falconer Mitchell.

Text

Box 3.3: Reproduced with permission of Accountancy Books; *Box 3.4:* Carr, R. (1996) 'Towards a truer measure of value', *Financial Times*, 11 December 1996; *Box 3.5:* Larsen, P. (1997) 'What's it all about, EVA', *Investor's Chronicle*, 17 January 1997, Financial Times Business Information; *Box 4.3:* NAO (1998) *The Privatisation of the Rolling Stock Leasing Companies*, 5 March 1998, The National Audit Office, HMSO. Parliamentary copyright material reproduced with the permission of the Controller of Her Majesty's Stationery Office on behalf of Parliament; pp. 40–54: Adapted and reprinted by permission of Paul Chapman Publishing from Bowerman, M. (1996) 'The rise and fall of value for money auditing', in *Accounting and Performance Measurement*, Lapsley, I. and Mitchell, F. Copyright © 1996 Irvine Lapsley and Falconer Mitchell; *Box 5.1:* Connon, H. (1998) 'Trackers trip up the top pension funds', *The Observer*, 5 May 1998; *Box 5.3:* Masterton, J. (1998) 'Shares in the action', *Financial Times*, 27 April 1998, Financial Times Syndication.

Every effort has been made to trace all copyright owners, but if any has been inadvertently overlooked, the publishers will be pleased to make the necessary arrangements at the first opportunity.

B821 Financial Strategy

BLOCK 1 INTRODUCTION
Unit 1 The Fundamentals of Finance

BLOCK 2 FINANCIAL APPRAISAL
Unit 2 Understanding Accounts
Unit 3 Forecasting Financial Performance

BLOCK 3 FINANCE AND INVESTMENT
Unit 4 Finance Tools
Unit 5 Project Appraisal
Unit 6 Company Appraisal

BLOCK 4 FINANCIAL RISK MANAGEMENT
Unit 7 Risk Assessment and Interest Rate Risk
Unit 8 Foreign Exchange and Trade Risk
Unit 9 Contingent Risk and Policy Issues

BLOCK 5 STRATEGIC IMPLICATIONS
Unit 10 Internal and External Finance